GRAMMAR essentials

for the Pre-GED Student

Laurie Rozakis, Ph.D.

THOMSON ™ — **ARCO**

Australia • Canada • Mexico • Singapore • Spain • United Kingdom • United States

An ARCO Book

ARCO is a registered trademark of Thomson Learning, Inc., and is used herein under license by Peterson's.

About The Thomson Corporation and Peterson's

The Thomson Corporation, with 2002 revenues of $7.8 billion, is a global leader in providing integrated information solutions to business and professional customers. The Corporation's common shares are listed on the Toronto and New York stock exchanges (TSX: TOC; NYSE: TOC). Its learning businesses and brands serve the needs of individuals, learning institutions, corporations, and government agencies with products and services for both traditional and distributed learning. Peterson's (www.petersons.com) is a leading provider of education information and advice, with books and online resources focusing on education search, test preparation, and financial aid. Its Web site offers searchable databases and interactive tools for contacting educational institutions, online practice tests and instruction, and planning tools for securing financial aid. Peterson's serves 110 million education consumers annually.

For more information, contact Peterson's, 2000 Lenox Drive, Lawrenceville, NJ 08648;
800-338-3282; or find us on the World Wide Web at: www.petersons.com/about

ISBN: 0-7689-1247-4

Printed in the United States of America

10 9 8 7 6 5 4 3 2 1   05 04 03

First Edition

Contents

Introduction   v

Section I   Evaluating Your Skills

       Pretest   **3**

Section II   Words: Parts of Speech

       1   **Nouns**   **9**

       2   **Verbs**   **19**

       3   **Pronouns**   **29**

       4   **Conjunctions**   **41**

Section III   Words: More Parts of Speech

       5   **Adjectives**   **53**

       6   **Adverbs**   **63**

       7   **Prepositions and Interjections**   **73**

Section IV   Sentences: Putting Words Together

       8   **Phrases**   **85**

       9   **Clauses**   **95**

       10   **Sentences**   **103**

Section V   Common Grammar Problems

11 **Correcting Sentence Errors   115**

12 **Agreement of Subject and Verb   125**

13 **Dangling and Misplaced Modifiers   135**

14 **Correcting Double Negatives   145**

Section VI   Mechanics

15 **Using Commas Correctly   155**

16 **Other Punctuation   165**

17 **Capitalization   175**

Section VII   Reevaluating Your Skills

Posttest   187

Section VIII   Appendices

A **About the GED   201**

B **Idiom List and Word Formation   207**

C **Test-Taking Tips and Strategies   227**

Introduction

You have taken a big step toward success on the GED Language Arts, Writing test by using this book. We know that you have a full, busy life and need a test-prep book that gives you fast and easy access to the skills that you need. We've created *Grammar Essentials for the Pre-GED Student* with that in mind.

People are judged on the way they use grammar. A grammatical error in your speech or writing can be embarrassing. Poor grammar in a document is like a stain on your jacket—people think you're sloppy. Making a lot of grammar mistakes can stand in your way of getting your message across, too.

What's great about grammar is that it *can* be learned, like any other skill worth knowing. Work through the lessons in this book and you'll have much more confidence when it comes to writing. It *is* worth the effort to learn the rules of grammar!

How to Study Grammar

Step #1 Complete one chapter at a time.

Step #2 Do all the quizzes in the chapter. Mark your answers.

Step #3 Go back and study the information that you got wrong.

Step #4 Take the Practice Test.

Step #5 Restudy anything you missed on the Practice Test.

About This Book

First, you're going to take the Pretest. The Pretest will help you figure out in which sections of the book you'll need to focus. The book is then divided into five review sections:

- Parts of speech

- More parts of speech

- Putting the words together into sentences

- Common grammar problems

- Mechanics

Each of these sections will teach you the grammar skills that you'll need to take the GED, including:

- Correcting sentence errors

- Agreement of subject and verb

- Correcting double negatives

- Using commas correctly

You'll also work with practice grammar drills in these review sections. After the review sections, you'll take the Posttest to see how much you have learned. Finally, we have included some test-taking tips and strategies in Appendix C to help you out on test day.

By the time we're finished, you'll be so confident in your grammar abilities, you won't need that computer grammar checker!

Let's get started.

Evaluating Your Skills

Pretest

The following sentences contain 10 errors in grammar. The errors include mistakes in:

- Phrases, clauses, and sentence structure
- Agreement of subject and verb
- Dangling and misplaced modifiers
- Punctuation
- Capitalization

Directions: Write the corrected sentence on the lines provided.

1. juliette gordon low started the girl scouts of america in 1912.

   Juliette Gordon Low started the Girl Scouts
   of America in 1912.

2. When she died in 1927, there was 168,000 Girl Scouts in the United States.

   _____

   _____

3. Today, there are more than 200,000 girls involved on Scouting into all levels.

   _____

   _____

4. Girl Scouts can meet other Girl Scouts at national centers from everywhere in the United States.

   _____

   _____

3

5. I like Girl Scouts, said little Shanta.

_____

_____

6. Where Juliette Gordon Low was born.

_____

_____

7. People can visit the historic house they can also learn about Juliette Gordon Low's life.

_____

_____

8. Girl Scout troops don't need no training to take part in many activities.

_____

_____

9. Girl Scouts can also meet at the Conference Center in Briarcliff Manor New York.

_____

_____

10. Adults meets to learn more about Girl Scouts.

_____

_____

Answers

The corrected errors are underlined.

1. <u>Juliette Gordon Low</u> started the <u>Girl Scouts</u> of <u>America</u> in 1912.

    Error in capitalization. (See Chapter 17)

2. When she died in 1927, <u>there were</u> 168,000 Girl Scouts in the United States.

    Error in agreement of subject and verb. (See Chapter 12)

3. Today, there are more than 200,000 girls involved <u>in</u> Scouting <u>on</u> all levels.

    Error in prepositions. (See Chapter 7)

4. Girl Scouts <u>from everywhere in the United States</u> can meet other Girl Scouts at national centers.

    Error in a misplaced modifier. (See Chapter 13)

5. <u>"</u>I like Girl Scouts<u>,"</u> said little Shanta.

    Error in quotation use. (See Chapter 16)

6. Juliette Gordon Low was born there.

    Error in sentence structure; this is a sentence fragment. (See Chapters 8, 9, 10, and 11)

7. People can visit the historic house<u>;</u> they can also learn about Juliette Gordon Low's life.

    Error in sentence structure; this is run-on sentence. (See Chapters 8, 9, 10, and 11)

8. Girl Scout troops don't need <u>any</u> training to take part in many activities.

    Error in double negatives. (See Chapter 14)

9. Girl Scouts can also meet at the Conference Center in Briarcliff Manor<u>,</u> New York.

    Error in comma use. (See Chapter 15)

10. Adults <u>meet</u> to learn more about Girl Scouts.

    Error in agreement of subject and verb. (See Chapter 12)

Words: Parts of Speech

Nouns | 1

English words are divided into eight different parts of speech according to the way they are used in a sentence. The parts of speech are:

- Nouns·
- Verbs
- Pronouns
- Conjunctions
- Adjectives
- Adverbs
- Prepositions
- Interjections

In this chapter, you will learn all about nouns.

What Is a Noun?

A *noun* is a word that names a person, place, or thing. Here are some examples:

Nouns That Name People	Nouns That Name Places	Nouns That Name Things
Vanna White	school	*The Scarlet Letter*
Juan Vincent	South America	shovel
child	Statue of Liberty	clouds

Nouns can name living things, nonliving things, ideas, conditions, and qualities. Here are some more examples:

Living Things	Nonliving Things	Ideas	Conditions	Qualities
snake	rock	justice	peace	courage
bird	scooter	honor	happiness	pride
cat	bus	mercy	sorrow	fear

Quick Quiz A

Directions: Arrange the following nouns on the chart, according to their category.

brick   San Juan   Bob   anxiety

Texans   kindness   Moscow   Charles   library

People	Places	Things/Conditions/Qualities
_____	_____	_____
_____	_____	_____
_____	_____	_____

Quick Quiz B

Directions: Underline the nouns in each sentence. The number in the parentheses ( ) tells you how many nouns are in each sentence.

1. People like to explore strange lands. (2)
2. Some explorers seek wealth and fame. (3)
3. Others study animals, plants, and people. (3)
4. Some people explore in ships on the ocean. (3)
5. Astronauts travel on spaceships into the galaxy. (3)

Nouns can be divided into four types: *common nouns, proper nouns, compound nouns,* and *collective nouns.*

Common Nouns and Proper Nouns

Common nouns name any one of a class of person, place, or thing.

Examples of Common Nouns		
man	country	cars
dog	food	computer

Proper nouns name a specific person, place, or thing.

Examples of Proper Nouns		
Bernard	Hong Kong	Chevrolet
Fido	New York	Dell

Quick Quiz C

Directions: Underline the common and proper nouns in each sentence. The number in the parenthesis ( ) tells you how many nouns are in each sentence.

1. In 1527, Cabeza de Vaca sailed to Florida. (2)
2. He explored Texas, New Mexico, and Arizona. (3)
3. James Cook was another great explorer. (2)
4. He traveled around the world twice. (1)
5. In 1860, Robert Burke and John Wills explored Australia. (3)

Compound Nouns and Collective Nouns

Compound nouns are two or more nouns that function as a single unit. A compound noun can be two separate words, words joined by a hyphen, or two words combined. Examples:

Individual Words	Hyphenated Words	Combined Words
time capsule	ninety-nine	baseball

Collective nouns name groups of people or things. Examples:

team	family	herd
crowd	jury	clan

Quick Quiz D

Directions: Circle the compound or collective noun in each word group.

1.	kicked	audience	he
2.	want	blew	grandmother
3.	bubble bath	green	slowly
4.	committee	into	and
5.	but	smiling	seatbelt

Possessive Nouns

Nouns can show ownership of things, ideas, and personality traits. In grammar, ownership is called *possession.* Here are two ways to show possession:

The car that belongs to Jill.   Jill's car.

While both ways of showing possession are correct, we usually use the second way——Jill's car——because it is less wordy.

Apostrophes are used with the noun to show the possessive case. An apostrophe looks like this: '. Notice that the apostrophe is only on the first noun because this is the noun that shows ownership. Examples:

Things	Ideas	Personality Traits
Andre's coats	Carmen's opinion	Richard's intelligence
Mai's books	Kim's judgment	Fabio's kindness

In many languages other than English, the object that is possessed is named first, followed by the person or thing that possesses it. For example: *This is the office of Jean.* As a result, the way possessives are formed in English often poses problems for nonnative speakers. Therefore, if English is not your first language, pay special attention to this next section.

How to Form Possessive Nouns

Follow these rules to use possessive nouns correctly.

1. With singular nouns, add an apostrophe and an *s*.

not possessive	*possessive*
monkey	monkey's banana
baby	baby's toy
boss	boss's orders

Note: Often, people drop the *s* after the apostrophe in a singular possessive noun that ends in *-s*. This is perfectly acceptable. Examples:

OK	Just as OK
Charles's book	Charles' book
Wolfs's advice	Wolfs' advice

2. With plural nouns ending is *s*, add an apostrophe after the *s*.

not possessive	*possessive*
kings	kings' thrones
dancers	dancers' shoes
singers	singers' voices

3. With plural nouns not ending in *s*, add an apostrophe and an *s*.

not possessive	*possessive*
sheep	sheep's wool
children	children's mittens
feet	feet's smell

4. To form the possessive of a business name, joint owner, or compound noun, put an apostrophe and *s* after the <u>last</u> word.

not possessive	*possessive*
Jones and Cadet	Jones and Cadet's offices
Gilbert and Sullivan	Gilbert and Sullivan's operas
brother-in-law	brother-in-law's watch

Quick Quiz E

Directions: Underline the possessive noun in each sentence.

1. Switzerland's mountains are very steep.
2. The Matterhorn's peak is 14,692 feet high!
3. The explorers' dream was to climb the Matterhorn.
4. The cliff's rocky sides made climbing very difficult.
5. Annie Peck's gear was very heavy.
6. The wind's force was like a hurricane.

Quick Quiz F

Directions: Underline the correct possessive form for each phrase. The first one is done for you.

1. the ideas of Katy

    <u>Katy's ideas</u>   Katys' ideas

2. the roles of the actors

    actors' roles   actor's roles

3. the colors of the rainbow

    rainbows' colors   rainbow's colors

4. the anger of the toddler

    toddlers' anger   toddler's anger

5. the poems of Edgar Lee Masters

    Edgar Lee Master's poems   Edgar Lee Masters' poems

6. the water of the bathtub

    bathtub's water   bathtubs' water

7. the cheers of the fans

    fan's cheers   fans' cheers

8. the pledge of the Boy Scouts

    Boy Scout's pledge   Boy Scouts' pledge

9. the paints of the artist

    artists' paints   artist's paints

10. the helmets of the divers

    diver's helmets   divers' helmets

Answers to Quick Quizzes

Answers to Quick Quiz A

People	Places	Things/Conditions/Qualities
Texans	San Juan	brick
Charles	Moscow	kindness
Bob	library	anxiety

Answers to Quick Quiz B

1. People, lands
2. explorers, wealth, fame
3. animals, plants, people
4. people, ships, ocean
5. Astronauts, spaceships, galaxy

Answers to Quick Quiz C

1. Cabeza de Vaca, Florida
2. Texas, New Mexico, Arizona
3. James Cook, explorer
4. world
5. Robert Burke, John Wills, Australia

Answers to Quick Quiz D

1. audience
2. grandmother
3. bubble bath
4. committee
5. seatbelt

Answers to Quick Quiz E

1. Switzerland's
2. Matterhorn's
3. explorers'
4. cliff's
5. Peck's
6. wind's

Answers to Quick Quiz F

1. Katy's ideas
2. actors' roles
3. rainbow's colors
4. toddler's anger
5. Edgar Lee Masters' poems
6. bathtub's water
7. fans' cheers
8. Boy Scouts' pledge
9. artist's paints
10. divers' helmets

Practice Test

Directions: Underline the nouns in each sentence. The number in the parenthesis ( ) tells you how many nouns are in each sentence.

1. Butterflies and moths bring spring to life every year. (5)
2. They live on every continent except Antarctica. (2)
3. Most butterflies live near the Equator. (2)
4. They have a head, thorax, abdomen, but no backbone. (4)
5. Some butterflies live a week; others, about a year. (3)

Fill in each blank with a noun, as directed.

6. *common noun*   My favorite animal is a(n) _____.
7. *proper noun*   I wish I could travel to _____.
8. *compound noun*   For dinner, I like to eat _____.
9. *collective nouns*   I like to spend time with my _____.
10. *possessive noun*   My _____ favorite place is the beach.

Answers

1. Butterflies, moths, spring, life, year
2. continent, Antarctica
3. butterflies, Equator
4. head, thorax, abdomen, backbone
5. butterflies, week, year
6. Answers will vary.
7. Answers will vary.
8. Answers will vary.
9. Answers will vary.
10. Answers will vary.

Verbs | 2

Nouns and verbs are very important because they are the building blocks of every sentence. That is why you are learning about these two parts of speech in the beginning of this book. As you will learn in Chapter 10, every sentence must have a verb.

What Is a Verb?

Verbs are words that name an action or describe a state of being.

Examples of Verbs		
throw	was	exercise
strike	am	are
live	meet	will be

Quick Quiz A

Directions: Circle the verb in each word group. Look for the words that describe an action or a state of being.

1.	see	toe
2.	so	eats
3.	by	study
4.	was	into
5.	create	paper
6.	carrots	driving

There are four basic types of verbs: *action verbs, linking verbs, helping verbs,* and *verb phrases.*

Action Verbs

Action verbs tell what the subject does.

Examples of Action Verbs		
jump	kiss	laugh
bounce	nod	agree

The action can be something you can see. The action can also be a mental action, something you cannot see.

More Examples of Action Verbs	
Action You Can See	Action You Cannot See
gamble	learn
look	realize
swim	understand

Quick Quiz B

Directions: Arrange the following verbs on the chart, according to their category.

dreams	move	jumps
imagine	collapse	worry

Action You Can See	Action You Cannot See
_____	_____
_____	_____
_____	_____

Transitive and Intransitive Verbs

An action verb can be *transitive* or *intransitive. Transitive verbs* need a direct object. This means that a noun or pronoun must come after the verb. The noun or pronoun explains what the verb does.

To figure out if a verb is transitive, ask yourself, "Who?" or "What?" after the verb. If you can find an answer in the sentence, the verb is transitive. You need to understand transitive and intransitive verbs to write complete and correct sentences.

Below are some examples of transitive verbs. The transitive verb is underlined in each sentence.

Using Transitive Verbs Correctly		
Incorrect	Question	Correct
The player <u>dropped</u>	The player <u>dropped</u> what?	The player <u>dropped</u> the ball.
Jane <u>picked</u>	Jane <u>picked</u> what?	Jane <u>picked</u> up the ball.

Intransitive verbs do not need a direct object. Below are some examples. The intransitive verb is underlined in each sentence.

- What <u>broke</u>?
- Water <u>dripped</u> from the faucet.
- The temperature <u>fell</u> during the night.

Quick Quiz C

Directions: Arrange the following verbs on the chart, according to their category.

walks   decide   met

left   ate   looks

Transitive Verbs	Intransitive Verbs
_____	_____
_____	_____
_____	_____

Quick Quiz D

Directions: Label each underlined verb as "transitive" or "intransitive." Write your answer in the space provided.

_____   **1.** The cook <u>mixed</u> the butter into the eggs.

_____   **2.** Mother asked, "Who <u>called</u>?"

_____   **3.** The beautiful princess <u>kissed</u> the green frog.

_____   **4.** The slimy frog <u>turned</u> into a handsome prince!

_____   **5.** Luc <u>congratulated</u> the newlyweds.

_____   **6.** Because the road was so slippery, the jogger <u>tripped.</u>

Linking Verbs

Linking verbs join the subject and the predicate.

- A *subject* tells who or what the sentence is about. The subject is a noun or a pronoun.
- A *predicate* tells what the subject is or does. The *verb* is found in the predicate.

You will learn more about subjects and predicates in Chapter 10.

Linking verbs do not show action. Instead, they help the words at the end of the sentence name and describe the subject. All forms of *to be* are linking verbs. These include:

Forms of *To Be*			
am	are	is	was
were	am being	are being	is being
was being	were being	can be	could be
may be	might be	must be	shall be
should be	will be	would be	have been
had been	could have been	may have been	might have been
must have been	shall have been	should have been	

Here are the other common linking verbs:

Common Linking Verbs			
appear	be	become	feel
grow	look	remain	seem
smell	sound	stay	taste

Although small in size as well as number, linking verbs are used often. Below are two examples. The linking verb is underlined in each sentence.

- The assistant <u>was</u> happy about the job change.
- She <u>is</u> now making more money.

Quick Quiz E

Directions: Circle the linking verb in each word group.

1.	jogs		is
2.	sweater		remain
3.	was		nose
4.	seem		eyes
5.	me		had been
6.	five		taste

Quick Quiz F

Directions: Underline the linking verb in each sentence.

1. The television sounded loud in the small room.

2. The food tasted odd, even to those used to his weird cooking.

3. The road seemed to shimmer in the extreme heat.

4. It looked watery, too, as though flooded.

5. The ducks remained quiet, not fooled by the shimmer.

6. We were happy to take a vacation, even though it was brief.

Many linking verbs can also be used as action verbs. Here is an example using the verb *looked*:

- *Linking verb:*　The puppy *looked* sad.
- *Action verb:*　I *looked* for the lost puppy.

To figure out whether a verb is being used as a linking verb or an action verb, replace it with *am, are,* or *is.* If the sentence makes sense with the substitution, the original verb is a linking verb.

Helping Verbs

Helping verbs are added to another verb to make the meaning clearer. Helping verbs include any form of *to be.* Here are the most common helping verbs:

Helping Verbs			
can	could	did	do
does	had	has	have
may	might	must	shall
should	will	would	

Quick Quiz G

Directions: Circle the helping verb in each word group. Look for forms of the verb *to be*.

1.	skips	should
2.	meets	might
3.	sleeping	did
4.	drive	do
5.	sing	does
6.	would	overnight

Verb phrases are made of one main verb and one or more helping verbs. Below are two examples. The verb phrase is underlined in each sentence:

- They <u>will run</u> after dinner.
- They <u>do have</u> fun staying fit.

Answers to Quick Quizzes

Answers to Quick Quiz A

1. see
2. eats
3. study
4. was
5. create
6. driving

Answers to Quick Quiz B

Action You Can See	Action You Cannot See
jumps	imagine
collapse	worry
move	dreams

Answers to Quick Quiz C

Transitive Verbs	Intransitive Verbs
met	left
ate	looks
walks	decide

Answers to Quick Quiz D

1. transitive
2. intransitive
3. transitive
4. transitive
5. transitive
6. intransitive

Answers to Quick Quiz E

1. is
2. remain
3. was
4. seem
5. had been
6. taste

Answers to Quick Quiz F

1. sounded
2. tasted
3. seemed
4. looked
5. remained
6. were

Answers to Quick Quiz G

1. should
2. might
3. did
4. do
5. does
6. would

Practice Test

Directions: Underline the verb in each sentence.

1. I study hard for the GED.
2. Jean is the hardest worker.
3. These tacos taste great.
4. I am nervous about the GED.
5. My sister shouted for me.
6. The milk smells fresh.
7. The big sale was great.
8. We felt happier after lunch.
9. Who read this book?
10. The book fell off the shelf.

Directions: Write a verb in each blank to complete the sentence.

11. A small boat _____ on the horizon.
12. It _____ larger and larger as it flew closer.
13. The object _____ to be made from shiny metal.
14. The pizza _____ burned, and no one wanted to eat it.
15. However, it _____ fine, if a bit crisp and chewy.
16. Who _____ that stranger I saw you talking to yesterday?
17. Lacey _____ the winner.
18. The Fitzpatricks _____ great neighbors.

Answers

1. study
2. is
3. taste
4. am
5. shouted
6. smells
7. was
8. felt
9. read
10. fell

Possible Answers

11. appears, appeared
12. became
13. seemed
14. smelled
15. tasted, was
16. was
17. is, was
18. are

Pronouns 3

Read these sentences:

Mr. Ramirez gave Mr. Ramirez's book to Mr. Ramirez's wife, Mrs. Ramirez. Mrs. Ramirez read the book after dinner.

Sounds pretty silly, doesn't it? That's because the writer used the proper noun "Ramirez" over and over. Here's what the same sentence looks like with **pronouns** used in place of some of the nouns:

Mr. Ramirez gave <u>his</u> book to <u>his</u> wife. <u>She</u> read the book after dinner.

Pronouns help you write graceful and logical sentences. Pronouns help you get rid of nouns that you have used over and over.

What Is a Pronoun?

A pronoun is a word used in place of a noun or another pronoun. Here are some pronouns:

		Examples of Pronouns		
I	you	he	she	who
his	it	mine	your	whom

Quick Quiz A

Directions: Circle the pronoun in each word group.

1.	book	their
2.	watch	they
3.	who	New Mexico
4.	me	for
5.	and	we
6.	skips	I

What Is an Antecedent?

A pronoun gets its meaning from the noun for which it stands. That noun is called the *antecedent.* Here is an example:

> Although <u>ice cream</u> is fattening, <u>it</u> is my favorite snack food.

The *antecedent* is "ice cream" and the pronoun is "it."

Quick Quiz B

Directions: Circle the antecedent in each sentence. Make sure you look for nouns. The pronoun is underlined for you.

1. Lee usually brings <u>his</u> breakfast to work.
2. The dog stayed in <u>its</u> bed.
3. Ricardo enjoyed <u>himself</u> on vacation.
4. Did Debbie bring <u>her</u> brownies?
5. The travelers loaded <u>their</u> bags into the car.
6. Orlando is my favorite city because of <u>its</u> amusement parks.

Personal Pronouns and Possessive Pronouns

Personal pronouns refer to a specific person, place, object, or thing. The following chart shows all the personal pronouns:

Personal Pronouns		
	Singular (One)	*Plural* (More than One)
first-person	I, me, mine, my	we, us, our, ours
second-person	you, your, yours	you, your, yours
third-person	he, him, his, she, her, hers, it	they, them, their, theirs, its

Possessive pronouns show ownership. (Remember in Chapter 1 we discussed possessive nouns.) The possessive pronouns are:

Possessive Pronouns			
yours	his	hers	whose
its	ours	theirs	

Quick Quiz C

Directions: Replace each underlined noun with a personal or possessive pronoun. Choose from the pronouns in the parentheses ( ). Write your answer on the line. The first is done for you.

1. John took <u>John's</u> (his/he) __his__ sweater to the cleaners.

2. The group took <u>the group's</u> (who/their) _____ picture by the Great Wall of China.

3. Louise took <u>Louise's</u> (her/it) _____ daughter out for ice cream after dinner.

4. When our friends bought a bookcase, we helped <u>our friends</u> (them/their) _____ move it in.

5. Barry had never eaten octopus before, but <u>Barry</u> (she/he) _____ tasted it anyway.

6. Ellen can read Spanish, but she is afraid to speak <u>Spanish</u> (it/who) _____.

7. I called my mother at work, but <u>my mother</u> (its/she) _____ was in a meeting.

8. Joe and Mary chose red and blue as <u>Joe and Mary's</u> (them/their) _____ party colors.

9. My parents took their trailer with <u>my parents</u> (them/whose) _____ on vacation.

10. If Mary comes to the party, I'll introduce <u>Mary</u> (him/her)_____ to my cousin.

Reflexive Pronouns and Intensive Pronouns

Reflexive pronouns add information to a sentence by pointing back to a noun or pronoun that is near the beginning of the sentence. Reflexive pronouns end in *-self* or *-selves*. The pronouns are used this way in a sentence:

- Christa bought <u>herself</u> a new car.
- Her family enjoyed <u>themselves</u> driving in her car.

Intensive pronouns also end in *-self* or *-selves,* but they just add emphasis to the noun or pronoun. The pronouns are used this way in a sentence:

- Christa <u>herself</u> paid for the car.
- She said that she would be able to afford the car <u>herself.</u>

Quick Quiz D

Directions: Circle the reflexive pronoun or the intensive pronoun in each word group.

1.	me	myself
2.	itself	it
3.	you	ourselves
4.	whom	yourselves
5.	herself	her
6.	he	himself

Demonstrative Pronouns

Demonstrative pronouns direct attention to a specific person, place, or thing. There are only four demonstrative pronouns:

Demonstrative Pronouns	
Singular (One)	*Plural* (More than One)
this	these
that	those

The following sentences show how demonstrative pronouns are used. The demonstrative pronoun is underlined in each sentence:

- <u>This</u> is the movie we want to see.
- <u>That</u> is my favorite car.
- <u>These</u> are my boots.
- <u>Those</u> are the candies I like.

Quick Quiz E

Directions: Circle the demonstrative pronoun in each sentence.

1. Is this my seat?
2. That is a beautiful cat!
3. It seems like these guests will never leave!
4. Those pants are too tight.
5. This fish is delicious.
6. Where did you put that folder?

Relative Pronouns

Relative pronouns begin a subordinate clause or part of the sentence. A relative pronoun links a complete sentence to part of a sentence. There are only five relative pronouns:

Relative Pronouns		
that	which	who
whom	those	

The following sentences show how relative pronouns are used. The relative pronoun is underlined in each sentence.

Lisa bought the dress	<u>that</u> she saw in the ad.
Complete sentence	**subordinate clause**

I sold my car,	<u>which</u> was fifteen years old.
Complete sentence	**subordinate clause**

Harry is the player	<u>who</u> caught the touchdown.
Complete sentence	**subordinate clause**

Interrogative Pronouns

Interrogative pronouns ask a question. Most relative pronouns can be used as interrogative pronouns, too. These five interrogative pronouns are used in English:

Interrogative Pronouns		
what	which	who
whom	whose	

The following sentences show how interrogative pronouns are used. The interrogative pronoun is underlined in each sentence:

- <u>What</u> do you want?
- <u>Which</u> bus do you take?
- <u>Who</u> misplaced the remote control?
- With <u>whom</u> do you wish to speak?
- <u>Whose</u> newspaper is on the floor?

Quick Quiz F

Directions: Circle the relative pronoun or interrogative pronoun in each word group.

1.	who	I
2.	me	whose
3.	which	go
4.	nice	what
5.	whom	you
6.	lucky	that

Indefinite Pronouns

Indefinite pronouns refer to people, places, objects, or things without pointing to a specific one. "In" means *not*. These pronouns are called "indefinite" because they do not name a definite person, place, or thing. The following chart lists some of the most common indefinite pronouns.

Examples of Indefinite Pronouns			
Singular	**Plural**	**Singular or Plural**	
another	nobody	both	all
anyone	nothing	few	any
each	other	many	more
everyone	someone	others	most
everybody	anybody	several	none
everything	anything	some	
no one	one		

The following sentences show how indefinite pronouns are used. The indefinite pronoun is underlined in each sentence:

- <u>Everyone</u> wants to get on the subway.

- <u>Many</u> people are shoving and pushing.

- <u>All</u> the cars are filled.

Using Pronouns Correctly

Always remember that a pronoun replaces a noun. To make sure that your writing is clear, always use the noun <u>before</u> you use the pronoun. To make your sentences clear, follow these three rules:

- Make a pronoun clearly refer to a single antecedent.

- Place pronouns close to their antecedents.

- Make a pronoun refer to a definite antecedent.

Answers to Quick Quizzes

Answers to Quick Quiz A

1. their
2. they
3. who
4. me
5. we
6. I

Answers to Quick Quiz B

1. Lee
2. dog
3. Ricardo
4. Debbie
5. travelers
6. Orlando

Answers to Quick Quiz C

1. his
2. their
3. her
4. them
5. he
6. it
7. she
8. their
9. them
10. her

Answers to Quick Quiz D

1. myself
2. itself
3. ourselves
4. yourselves
5. herself
6. himself

Answers to Quick Quiz E

1. this
2. That
3. these
4. Those
5. This
6. that

Answers to Quick Quiz F

1. who
2. whose
3. which
4. what
5. whom
6. that

Practice Test

Directions: Underline the pronoun in each sentence.

1. I go to sleep early.

2. Mike made himself a hot dog.

3. This is the best game!

4. Anyone seen my eyeglasses?

5. Please bring your CDs to the party.

6. The guests poured themselves some punch.

7. Casey bought those pants?

8. Ling had to weed her mother's garden.

9. She likes to be in the sunlight.

10. Betty put up the volleyball net herself.

Answers

1. I
2. himself
3. This
4. Anyone
5. your
6. themselves
7. those
8. her
9. She
10. herself

Conjunctions 4

You have already learned about nouns and verbs, the building blocks of sentences. You also learned how pronouns can be used in place of nouns. In this chapter, you will learn about *conjunctions*. They are used to join words or sentences.

What Is a Conjunction?

Conjunctions connect words or groups of words and show how they are related to one another. Here are some examples:

Examples of Conjunctions		
and	but	since
because	so	after
than	although	for

Quick Quiz A

Directions: Circle the conjunction in each word group. Look for the words that can be used to link ideas.

1.	house	and
2.	although	dog
3.	runs	because
4.	since	swims
5.	I	than
6.	so	you
7.	snow	but
8.	after	allow
9.	job	for
10.	him	or

There are three kinds of conjunctions: *coordinating conjunctions, correlative conjunctions*, and *subordinating conjunctions*. Let's look at each one.

Coordinating Conjunctions

Coordinating conjunctions link words or word groups. The words have to fit together so the sentence makes sense. There are only eight coordinating conjunctions:

The Seven Coordinating Conjunctions			
and	but	for	not
nor	or	so	yet

Use the following memory trick to help you remember the seven coordinating conjunctions:

FANBOYS

Each letter of FANBOYS stands for the first letter of one of the coordinating conjunctions. Study the following:

For

And

Nor

But

Or

Yet

So

Quick Quiz B

Directions: Complete this puzzle by writing the coordinating conjunction that starts with each letter. You should write in 1 letter for each line.

F _ _   A _ _ _   N _ _   B _ _   O _   Y _ _   S _

How to Use Coordinating Conjunctions

As you have just learned, coordinating conjunctions link words or word groups. Coordinating conjunctions can link many different words and word groups. Here are some examples:

- Coordinating conjunctions can link nouns.

  Here is an example. The coordinating conjunction is underlined.

  My father <u>and</u> mother went to the dance.

      noun   noun

- Coordinating conjunctions can link verbs.

  Here is an example. The coordinating conjunction is underlined.

  The cat fell <u>but</u> landed feet down.

      verb   verb

- Coordinating conjunctions can link pronouns.

  Here is an example. The coordinating conjunction is underlined.

  Give the package to him <u>or</u> her.

      pronoun   pronoun

- Coordinating conjunctions can link other word groups.

  Here are some examples. The coordinating conjunctions are under lined.

  He made a simple <u>yet</u> delicious dinner.

  Put the box on the table <u>or</u> on the floor.

- Coordinating conjunctions can link two or more sentences.

  Here is an example. The coordinating conjunction is underlined.

  I did not do the laundry, <u>so</u> my husband did it himself.

Quick Quiz C

Directions: Underline the coordinating conjunction in each sentence.

1. Police officers and detectives solve crimes.
2. They work hard but like their jobs.
3. Do you prefer Sherlock Holmes or Dick Tracy?
4. They are make-believe yet seem real.
5. All detectives use clues so they can find out the truth.
6. We will never support crime nor anyone who does.

Quick Quiz D

Directions: Complete each sentence with a coordinating conjunction. Choose the conjunction that makes the most sense in the sentence.

1. We are born with 300 bones, (yet/nor) _____ 100 of those bones grow together.

2. Only elephants (and/yet)_____ humans are afraid when they see old bones.

3. Bones are important (for/or) _____ they make blood cells.

4. Bones are strong (nor/but) _____ they can break easily.

5. I have never seen my bones (nor/yet) _____ anyone else's bones.

6. Bones (but/and)_____ muscles help us move.

7. Some bones are large (or/yet) _____ others are very, very small.

8. Our organs are protected by bones, (but/or) _____organs can still get hurt.

9. Did you break your arm (or/but) _____ your leg?

10. Bones are important (so/nor) _____ you better take care of yours!

Correlative Conjunctions

Like coordinating conjunctions, *correlative conjunctions* link similar words or word groups. But unlike coordinating conjunctions, correlative conjunctions are always used in pairs. If you use the first word in the pair, you must use the second word in the pair. Here are the correlative conjunctions:

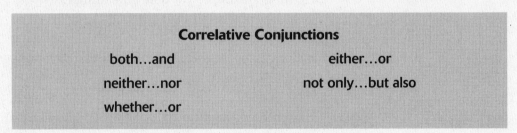

Correlative Conjunctions

both…and   either…or

neither…nor   not only…but also

whether…or

Below are some examples. The correlative conjunctions are underlined:

* She found <u>both</u> the beach <u>and</u> the campgrounds.
* <u>Either</u> you come with us now, <u>or</u> you will miss the bus.
* <u>Neither</u> the cars <u>nor</u> the trucks could get through the snow.

Quick Quiz E

Directions: Complete each correlative conjunction by writing the missing word.

1. both…_____
2. either…_____
3. neither…_____
4. not only…_____
5. whether…_____
6. _____…and
7. _____…or
8. _____…nor
9. _____…but also
10. _____…or

Subordinating Conjunctions

Subordinating conjunctions link a complete sentence (or independent clause) to a fragment (dependent clause). There are *many* subordinating conjunctions. Here are the subordinating conjunctions that are used most often:

Subordinating Conjunctions	
after	as if
although	as long as
as	as soon as
because	as though
before	even though
if	in order that
since	so, so that
though	till
when	unless
whenever	until
where	wherever

Subordinating conjunctions can be used in the beginning of a sentence or the middle of a sentence. Below are some examples. The subordinating conjunctions are underlined.

Subordinating conjunction at the beginning of a sentence:

- <u>Since</u> the rain started, we have had floods.
- <u>Unless</u> you have a better idea, let's use my plan.

Subordinating conjunction in the middle of a sentence:

- You will have to call after lunch <u>because</u> no one is here now.
- Please set the table <u>while</u> I make the pasta.

Quick Quiz F

Directions: Circle the subordinating conjunction in each word group.

1.	because	mouse
2.	sleep	although
3.	before	you
4.	seven	if
5.	cousin	since
6.	unless	turkey

Answers to Quick Quizzes

Answers to Quick Quiz A

1. and
2. although
3. because
4. since
5. than
6. so
7. but
8. after
9. for
10. or

Answers to Quick Quiz B

for,   and,   nor,   but,   or,   yet,   so

Answers to Quick Quiz C

1. and
2. but
3. or
4. yet
5. so
6. nor

Answers to Quick Quiz D

1. yet
2. and
3. for
4. but
5. nor
6. and
7. yet
8. but
9. or
10. so

Answers to Quick Quiz E

1. and
2. or
3. nor
4. but also
5. or
6. both
7. either
8. neither
9. not only
10. whether

Answers to Quick Quiz F

1. because
2. although
3. before
4. if
5. since
6. unless

Practice Test

Directions: Underline the conjunction or pair of conjunctions in each sentence.

1. Trees are not only beautiful but also useful.

2. Trees give us shade and food.

3. When you plant trees, your home gets shade.

4. Trees are home to many animals because they give shelter.

5. Trees have leaves or needles.

6. I like trees so I planted many in my yard.

7. Before you plant a tree, you must check the soil.

8. Even though trees are large, they can be damaged.

9. Both pines and firs grow in my yard.

10. Trees are found everywhere on Earth but the South Pole.

Answers

1. not only…but also
2. and
3. when
4. because
5. or
6. so
7. Before
8. Even though
9. Both…and
10. but

Words: More Parts of Speech

Adjectives 5

In this chapter and the next, you will learn about adjectives and adverbs. Both adjectives and adverbs are called "modifiers" because they modify (change) a word by describing it.

What Is an Adjective?

Adjectives are words that describe nouns and pronouns. Here are some examples:

The clown had a <u>red</u> nose.
            adjective   noun

This is his <u>first</u> show.
       adjective   noun

You   were <u>generous</u> to share your sandwich.
pronoun   adjective

She   was <u>right.</u>
pronoun   adjective

You can tell that a word is an adjective if it answers one of these four questions:

- What kind?
- How much?
- Which one?
- How many?

Read the following examples. The adjective is underlined in each example.

How to Identify Adjectives			
What kind	**How much?**	**Which one?**	**How many?**
<u>sick</u> puppy	<u>enough</u> money	<u>that</u> drink	<u>one</u> cookie
<u>green</u> car	<u>more</u> salt	<u>second</u> chance	<u>several</u> apples
<u>gold</u> ring	<u>little</u> effort	<u>any</u> friend	<u>six</u> buttons

As these examples show, the adjective usually comes *before* the noun or pronoun. However, the adjective may also come *after* the noun or pronoun.

Quick Quiz A

Directions: Complete the chart by writing an adjective that answers each question.

What kind?		How much?	
diamond	ring	_another_	time
cold	water	_more_	flour
nice	friend	_better_	effort

Which one?		How many?	
that	muffin	_several_	clouds
first	choice	_many_	guests
his	child	_different_	viewpoints

Quick Quiz B

Directions: Circle the adjective in each word group. Look for the words that could be used to describe a noun or pronoun.

1.	pink	tiger
2.	me	steady
3.	and	some
4.	cold	but
5.	Lucy	any
6.	raw	you

There are four basic kinds of adjectives: *common adjectives, proper adjectives, compound adjectives,* and *articles.* Let's look at each one.

Common Adjectives

Common adjectives describe nouns or pronouns. Below are some examples. The adjective is underlined in each phrase.

Common Adjectives	
<u>strong</u> will	<u>big</u> fence
<u>pretty</u> sunset	<u>good</u> show

Quick Quiz C

Directions: Underline the common adjective in each sentence.

1.   Animals and people adapt to cold weather in different ways.
2.   Polar bears have thick fat.
3.   They also have heavy fur.
4.   The red bat sleeps during the winter.
5.   Toads hide deep underground.
6.   Fishermen wear warm clothes.

Proper Adjectives

Proper adjectives are formed from proper nouns. Below are some examples. The adjective is underlined in each phrase.

<u>California</u> lettuce   <u>Bush</u> cabinet

<u>Italian</u> food   <u>French</u> bread

Quick Quiz D

Directions: Circle the proper adjective in each sentence. Look for the describing words that are capitalized.

1.   We planted Dutch tulips in the garden.
2.   My sister bought a French poodle.
3.   The poodle didn't like the Florida sunshine.
4.   My neighbor has an Irish setter.
5.   We ate a Greek salad for lunch.
6.   It tastes good with Spanish rice.

Compound Adjectives

Compound adjectives are made up of more than one word. Below are some examples. The adjective is underlined in each phrase.

Compound Adjectives

<u>hard-shell</u> crab   <u>high-pitched</u> sound

<u>nearsighted</u> child   <u>hard-working</u> person

Quick Quiz E

Directions: Circle the compound adjective in each phrase. Look for adjectives that are made of two words. These words may or may not have a hyphen (-).

1. far-off country
2. hard-boiled egg
3. nearby restaurant
4. farsighted adult
5. color-blind cat
6. low-pitched sound

Articles

Articles are a special type of adjective. There are three articles: *a, an,* and *the:*

- *The* is called a "definite article" because it refers to a specific thing.

- *A* and *an* are called "indefinite articles" because they refer to general things.

Special Rules for Using A and An

The indefinite articles *a* and *an* are grammatically the same. They both mean "one of many." However, there are special rules for using *a* and *an.* Here are the rules:

1. Use *a* and *an* only with singular nouns. "Singular" means *one.*

    a television   an apple

2. Use *a* when the word that follows begins with a consonant sound. Here are some examples:

    a cat   a park   a table

    a palm tree   a plate   a vacation

3. Use *an* before words that begin with vowel sounds. Here are some examples:

an essay   an elephant   an oyster

an honest person   an only child   an ugly dress

Quick Quiz F

Directions: Complete each sentence by selecting the correct article. Write your answer in the space provided for you.

1. Jesse bought (a/an) _____ new camera.

2. He needed (a/an) _____ roll of film.

3. Matthew has (a/an) _____ odd job.

4. It really is (a/an) _____ unusual occupation.

5. He is (a/an) _____ elephant trainer!

6. Jamal needs (a/an) _____ pencil.

7. Dr. Washington is (a/an) _____ honest man.

8. Ms. Chang is (a/an) _____ professor.

9. Today, she taught (a/an) _____ history lesson.

10. It was (a/an) _____ interesting class.

Special Rules for Using **The**

There are special rules for using *the*. Here are the rules:

1. Use *the* with specific singular and plural nouns.

I need *the* <u>frying pan.</u>   I need *the* <u>spoons</u>.

2. Use *the* with one-of -a-kind objects.

Look at *the* <u>moon</u>!   This is *the* <u>last</u> cookie.

3. Use *the* with the names of oceans, seas, rivers, and deserts.

the <u>Pacific Ocean</u>   *the* <u>Grand Canyon</u>

the <u>Sahara Desert</u>   *the* <u>Caribbean Sea</u>

4. Use *the* with the names of colleges and universities containing the word "of."

She studied at *the* <u>University of Florida</u>

Other times, nouns do not take the definite article *the*. Do not use *the* with the names of people, general positions, continents, states, cities, streets, religious place names, titles of officials, fields of study, names of diseases, or names of magazines and newspapers (unless it is part of the title).

Using Articles Correctly

Correct	Incorrect
George Bush	the George Bush
Europe	the Europe
Pennsylvania	the Pennsylvania
Green Street	the Green Street
heaven	the heaven
King Louis	the King Louis
math	the math
arthritis	the arthritis
Newsday	the *Newsday*
The Daily News (part of title)	

Quick Quiz G

Directions: Cross out the definite article "the" where it's *not* needed. The number in parentheses ( ) tells you how many "*the's*" to cross out.

1. John Chapman became known as "Johnny Appleseed" for planting the apple trees in the Midwest. (1)

2. He planted trees in the Ohio and the Illinois. (2)

3. He planted trees in the Indiana, too. (1)

4. The Johnny Appleseed did this when the United States was new. (1)

Answers to Quick Quizzes

Possible Answers to Quick Quiz A

What kind?	How much?	Which one?	How many?
silver ring	much time	this muffin	few clouds
hot water	some flour	first choice	many guests
good friend	added effort	third child	different viewpoints

Answers to Quick Quiz B

1. pink
2. steady
3. some
4. cold
5. any
6. raw

Answers to Quick Quiz C

1. cold
2. thick
3. heavy
4. red
5. deep
6. warm

Answers to Quick Quiz D

1. Dutch
2. French
3. Florida
4. Irish
5. Greek
6. Spanish

Answers to Quick Quiz E

1. far-off
2. hard-boiled
3. nearby
4. farsighted
5. color-blind
6. low-pitched

Answers to Quick Quiz F

1. a
2. a
3. an
4. an
5. an
6. a
7. an
8. a
9. a
10. an

Answers to Quick Quiz G

The corrected sentences should look like this:

1. John Chapman became known as "Johnny Appleseed" for planting apple trees in the Midwest. (1)
2. He planted trees in Ohio and Illinois. (2)
3. He planted trees in Indiana, too. (1)
4. Johnny Appleseed did this when the United States was new. (1)

Practice Test

Directions: Underline the adjective in each sentence.

1. Last year, there was a big hurricane in town.
2. It was a terrible time.
3. Some people moved to safer places.
4. Other people stayed in their wet homes.
5. They heard the strong winds.
6. Brave workers rescued them.

Directions: Write an adjective to complete each sentence.

7. Luc bought a _____new_____ jacket.
8. It matches his _____shiny_____ shoes.
9. We like to eat _____spicy_____ food.
10. Did you find _____that_____ store?
11. I lost _____one_____ mitten yesterday.
12. I'm glad I did not lose _____an_____ earring!

Answers

1. big
2. terrible
3. safer
4. wet
5. strong
6. brave

Possible Answers

7. red
8. new
9. Italian
10. the
11. a
12. an

Adverbs 6

As you learned in Chapter 5, *adjectives* and *adverbs* are the same in one way because they are both words that *describe*. But remember that *adjectives* and *adverbs* are also different because they are used to describe *different* parts of speech. Use this handy chart:

Adjectives Describe	Adverbs Describe
nouns	verbs
pronouns	adjectives
adverbs	

What Is an Adverb?

Adverbs are words that describe verbs, adjectives, or other adverbs. Read the following examples. The adverb and verb are underlined in each example:

- Adverb describing a verb:

  The package <u>arrived</u>   <u>today</u>.

     verb   adverb

- Adverb describing an adjective:

  Joanne looked <u>unusually</u> <u>pale</u>.

    adverb   adjective

- Adverb describing another adverb:

  The storm struck <u>very</u> <u>rapidly</u>.

    adverb   adverb

You can tell that a word is an adverb if it answers one of these four questions:

- When?
- Where?
- How?
- To what extent?

Read the following examples. The adjective is underlined in each example.

When?	Where?	How?	To What Extent?
left <u>yesterday</u>	fell <u>below</u>	danced <u>badly</u>	<u>partly</u> finished
begin <u>now</u>	move <u>up</u>	<u>happily</u> sang	eat <u>completely</u>

Quick Quiz A

Directions: Complete the chart by writing an adverb that answers each question.

When?	Where?
arrived _____	dropped _____
end _____	scattered _____
start _____	darkened _____

How?	To What Extent?
sang _____	_____ ripened
behaved _____	_____ recovered
walked _____	wash _____

Recognizing Adverbs

Look back at the chart. What do the adverbs *badly, happily, partly,* and *completely* have in common? That's right! They all end in *-ly.* Most adverbs are formed by adding *-ly* to an adjective. This makes recognizing an adverb fairly easy. Here are some examples:

Adverbs Formed by Adding *-ly* to an Adjective	
Adjective	Adverb
gentle	gently
slow	slowly
bright	brightly
swift	swiftly
nice	nicely

However, many adverbs do not end in *-ly.* Here are some of the most common adverbs that don't take the *-ly* ending.:

Adverbs that Do Not End in *-ly*	
afterward	almost
already	back
even	far
fast	hard
here	how
late	long
low	more
near	never
next	now
often	quick
rather	slow
so	soon
still	today
tomorrow	too
then	when
where	yesterday

Quick Quiz B

Directions: Circle the adverb in each word group. Look for the words that could be used to describe a verb, adverb, or adjective.

1.	tree	quickly
2.	nearly	flake
3.	we	especially
4.	very	they
5.	almost	him
6.	ran	completely
7.	slowly	jogged
8.	ski	seldom
9.	gently	nose
10.	sleep	poorly

Conjunctive Adverbs

Conjunctive adverbs are used to connect other words. Therefore, conjunctive adverbs act like conjunctions, but they are still adverbs. Conjunctive adverbs are also called *transitions* because they link ideas. The following chart lists the most common conjunctive adverbs:

<table>
<tr><th colspan="2">Conjunctive Adverbs</th></tr>
<tr><td>accordingly</td><td>again</td></tr>
<tr><td>also</td><td>consequently</td></tr>
<tr><td>besides</td><td>finally</td></tr>
<tr><td>however</td><td>for example</td></tr>
<tr><td>indeed</td><td>furthermore</td></tr>
<tr><td>moreover</td><td>on the other hand</td></tr>
<tr><td>nevertheless</td><td>otherwise</td></tr>
<tr><td>therefore</td><td>then</td></tr>
</table>

Quick Quiz C

Directions: Circle the conjunctive adverb in each word group. Look for the words that could be used to link ideas.

1.	moose	for example
2.	consequently	eggs
3.	myself	moreover
4.	however	zero
5.	rice	finally
6.	leaps	furthermore

The following examples show how conjunctive adverbs are used to link ideas. The conjunctive adverb is underlined in each sentence.

Peter likes the movies; <u>however,</u> he will only watch action films.
conjunctive adverb

The bus is unreliable; <u>for example,</u> it is usually twenty minutes late.
conjunctive adverb

She lost her key; <u>consequently,</u> she had to wait outside.
conjunctive adverb

Quick Quiz D

Directions: Add a conjunctive adverb to each sentence. Choose from the conjunctive adverbs in parentheses ( ). Write your choice in the space provided.

1. You should arrive early; (on the other hand/then), _____ you don't want to arrive too early.

2. The directions were easy; (accordingly/otherwise), _____ Jack put the toy together quickly.

3. It is a great job; (indeed/however) _____, it is a pleasure to go to work.

4. Eating candy before meals will spoil your appetite; (besides/however) _____, it will harm your teeth.

5. You are my sister; (nevertheless/then) _____, you cannot borrow my new dress.

Telling Adjectives and Adverbs Apart

Some words can be both adjectives and adverbs. It depends on how they are used in a sentence. Below are some examples:

The word *early:*

Adverb	I <u>left</u> <u>early.</u>	Adjective	I had an <u>early</u> <u>meeting.</u>
	verb adverb		adjective noun

The word *hard:*

Adverb	I <u>worked</u> <u>hard</u>.	Adjective	It was a <u>hard</u> <u>job.</u>
	verb adverb		adjective noun

Good and *well* can be confusing because *well* can be an adverb and an adjective. It depends on how the words are used in a sentence. Here are some guidelines:

1. *Good* is always an adjective. Here are some examples:

    • You are a *good* person.

    • Chico bought a *good* sandwich

2. *Well* is an adjective used to describe good health. Here are some examples:

    • You look *well.*

    • You sound *well* after your recent cold.

3. *Well* is an adverb when it is used for anything else. Here are some examples:

    • You swim *well.*

    • The baby sleeps *well.*

Quick Quiz E

Directions: Add *good* or *well* to complete each sentence. Write your choice in the space provided.

1. If you study hard, you will do (good/well) _____ on the GED.
2. Since he broke his leg, John isn't feeling (good/well) _____.
3. Karen makes (good/well) _____ spaghetti.
4. We always have a (good/well) _____ time at her house.
5. That's because she cooks so (good/well) _____.

Answers to Quick Quizzes

Possible Answers to Quick Quiz A

When?	Where?
arrived early	dropped under
end next	scattered everywhere
starts now	darkened overhead
How?	**To What Extent?**
sang sweetly	partly ripened
behaved badly	fully recovered
walked briskly	wash immediately

Answers to Quick Quiz B

1. quickly
2. nearly
3. especially
4. very
5. almost
6. completely
7. slowly
8. seldom
9. gently
10. poorly

Answers to Quick Quiz C

1. for example
2. consequently
3. moreover
4. however
5. finally
6. furthermore

Answers to Quick Quiz D

1. on the other hand
2. accordingly
3. indeed
4. besides
5. nevertheless

Answers to Quick Quiz E

1. well
2. well
3. good
4. good
5. well

Practice Test

Directions: Underline the adverb in each sentence.

1. Ian quickly ran to the front door.

2. My husband snores loudly.

3. The rain came down heavily.

4. Margot sews and knits well.

5. The baby patted the dog gently.

6. The coin fell below the turnstile.

Directions: Write an adverb to complete each sentence.

7. Move _____ and stop blocking the road!

8. The movie will begin _____.

9. We _____ read the novel.

10. The teenagers danced _____.

11. Our neighbors are moving _____

12. Do you _____ understand the problem?

Answers

1. quickly
2. loudly
3. heavily
4. well
5. gently
6. below

Possible Answers

7. aside, quickly
8. then, later
9. happily, slowly
10. awkwardly, closely
11. away, far
12. fully, completely

Prepositions and Interjections 7

Prepositions and interjections have different functions in English:

- Prepositions link ideas.
- Interjections get our attention.

However, they are alike in one way: They are both very short words!

What Is a Preposition?

Prepositions are words that link a noun or a pronoun that follows it to another word in the sentence. Here are some of the most common prepositions:

Common Prepositions

about	around	behind
against	above	along
across	at	as
around	amid	before
after	below	between
beneath	beyond	but
beside	by	despite
down	during	except
for	from	inside
into	in	like
near	out	off
on	outside	over
onto	of	opposite
past	since	toward
through	under	until
upon	underneath	with

Quick Quiz A

Directions: Circle the preposition in each word group. Look for words that could link a noun or a pronoun to another word in the sentence.

1.	past	squirrel
2.	Ronald	off
3.	them	toward
4.	until	sliding
5.	is	of
6.	beneath	black
7.	slowly	about
8.	into	good
9.	well	through
10.	inside	Lawrence

Quick Quiz B

Directions: Circle the preposition in each sentence.

1. I saw a lizard on the rock.
2. We were in the forest.
3. The park is near the highway.
4. During the summer, we visit the park daily.
5. We sit beside the waterfall.
6. I like to travel with my family.

Compound prepositions are made of more than one word. Here are some examples:

Examples of Compound Prepositions	
according to	ahead of
apart from	as of
because of	in addition to
in front of	in spite of
instead of	next to
owing to	prior to

Compound prepositions must be used as one unit. You cannot change words.

Quick Quiz C

Directions: Complete each compound preposition with the correct word. Write your answer on the space provided for you.

1. because (of/in) _____
2. in spite (at/of) _____
3. according (to/of) _____
4. next (by/to) _____
5. ahead (of/at) _____
6. in front (on/of) _____
7. prior (in/to) _____
8. apart (from/to) _____
9. as (of/at) _____
10. in addition (to/as) _____

Prepositional Phrases

A *prepositional phrase* is a group of words starting with a preposition and ending with a noun or a pronoun. Here are some examples:

- <u>around</u>   the <u>block</u>
  preposition   noun

- <u>by</u>   <u>our</u> side
  preposition   pronoun

A prepositional phrase can be long or short. Below are some more short prepositional phrases. The preposition is underlined in each one.

Examples of Short Prepositional Phrases	
<u>near</u> the basement	<u>on</u> the wing
<u>under</u> the bed	<u>in</u> the door
<u>around</u> the corner	<u>next to</u> the store

However, prepositional phrases can be much longer. That's because you can add adjectives to describe the noun or pronoun. You can also add adverbs to describe the adjectives. Below are some long prepositional phrases. The preposition is underlined in each one.

Examples of Long Prepositional Phrases

<u>near</u> the little girl dancing happily

<u>on account of</u> his intense work schedule

<u>opposite</u> the gas station and convenience store

<u>on</u> the corner of Fifth Avenue and Main Street

Quick Quiz D

Directions: Circle the prepositional phrase in each sentence.

1. My job is near the subway.
2. We travel under a tunnel.
3. The actor stood next to the camera.
4. There is a parking spot near the door.
5. Don't fall into the mud puddle!
6. I can see the building through the fog.

Using Prepositions Correctly

Using prepositions can be difficult because many prepositional phrases are *idiomatic*. This means they work as a unit and do not always make logical sense. Here are some guidelines:

1. Use the preposition *in* before seasons of the year. Also use *in* with months and years not followed by specific dates. Below are some examples. The preposition is underlined in each one:
   - <u>in</u> the summer
   - <u>in</u> January
   - <u>in</u> 2003

2. Use the preposition *on* before days of the week, holidays, and months. Below are some examples. The preposition is underlined in each one:
   - <u>on</u> Wednesday
   - <u>on</u> Thanksgiving
   - <u>on</u> July 20th

3. *Like* is a preposition that means "similar to." Therefore, it is followed by an object (usually a noun or pronoun). Below are some examples. The preposition is underlined in each one:
   - <u>like</u> Viktor
   - <u>like</u> you
   - <u>like</u> me

4.   Below is a list of idiomatic prepositional phrases and examples. *Always* use these prepositional phrases as units. Do not substitute other prepositions.

Prepositional Phrases

Prepositional Phrases	Examples
acquainted with	SueAnn is acquainted with my friend Saul.
addicted to	I am addicted to cola.
agree on (a plan)	The group finally agreed on a plan.
agree to (someone else's proposal)	Did Sara agree to their plan?
angry at or about (a thing)	The workers are angry about the pay cut.
angry with (a person)	They are angry with the boss.
apply for (a job)	You should apply for a job.
approve of	Did she approve of the promotion?
consists of	The snack consists of raisins and peanuts.
contrasts with	The green grass contrasts with the blue sky.
convenient for	Is today convenient for you?
deal with	How do you deal with the cold weather?
depend on	We can depend on you.
differs from (something)	The city differs from the country.
differ with (a person)	I differ with your opinion.
displeased with	Karl is displeased with the suit.
fond of	We are all fond of ice cream.
grateful for (something)	The child was grateful for a new toy.
grateful to (someone)	We are grateful to the fire fighter.
identical with	This dress is identical with hers.
interested in	Drew is interested in history.
interfere with	Going out too much can interfere with your sleep!
object to	We object to extra work.
protects against	A coat protects against cold.
reason with	You can't reason with a child.
responsible for	I am responsible for your safety.
shocked at	We are shocked at your rudeness!
similar to	It is similar to a bad storm.
specialize in	The doctor specializes in heart illness.
take advantage of	Don't take advantage of us!
worry about	I worry about him.

What Is an Interjection?

Interjections are words that show strong emotion. Below are some examples. The interjection is underlined in each one:

- <u>Oh,</u> you startled me.
- <u>Yes</u>, I will drive you there.
- <u>Ouch</u>! That hurts!

Look back at these three examples. You will see that interjections are set off from the rest of the sentence with a comma or an exclamation mark. Here are some more examples. The interjection is underlined in each one:

- <u>Wow</u>! That is a beautiful suit!
- <u>Uh,</u> that's my dessert you are eating.
- <u>Hey</u>! You missed the exit road!

Answers to Quick Quizzes

Answers to Quick Quiz A

1. past
2. off
3. toward
4. until
5. of
6. beneath
7. about
8. into
9. through
10. inside

Answers to Quick Quiz B

1. on
2. in
3. near
4. During
5. beside
6. with

Answers to Quick Quiz C

1. because of
2. in spite of
3. according to
4. next to
5. ahead of
6. in front of
7. prior to
8. apart from
9. as of
10. in addition to

Answers to Quick Quiz D

1. near the subway
2. under a tunnel
3. next to the camera
4. near the door
5. into the mud puddle
6. through the fog

Practice Test

Directions: Circle the preposition in each sentence.

1. The airplane flew <u>toward</u> the airport.
2. Don't touch the flowers <u>in</u> the garden!
3. Put the cleaner <u>under</u> the cabinet.
4. The runners raced <u>down</u> the hill.
5. Will you <u>agree to</u> my idea?
6. The shopper was <u>shocked</u> at the high prices.

Directions: Complete each prepositional phrase with the correct word. Write the word in the space provided.

7. Please do not take advantage (of/in) _____ us.
8. Vitamin C may protect (against/by) _____ colds.
9. My mother-in-law does not interfere (near/with) _____ us.
10. The student objected (from/to) _____ the low grade.
11. Are you interested (around/in) _____ grammar?
12. I hope this arrangement is convenient (for/instead of) _____ you.
13. Are you acquainted (in/with) _____ my family?
14. Don't forget to apply (to/for) _____ the contest.
15. My sister is addicted (with/to) _____ candy and other snacks.
16. The strikers are angry (for/about) _____ the loss of overtime pay.

Answers

1. toward
2. in
3. under
4. down
5. agree to
6. shocked at
7. of
8. against
9. with
10. to
11. in
12. for
13. with
14. for
15. to
16. about

Sentences: Putting Words Together

Phrases 8

In this chapter and in the next two chapters, you will learn how to build sentences. You will start with the smallest unit of words, a *phrase*. Then you will learn about clauses and sentences.

What Is a Phrase?

A *phrase* is a group of words that acts in a sentence as a single part of speech. A phrase does not have a subject or a verb. As a result, a phrase cannot stand alone. It *must* be added to another group of words. Here are some phrases:

Examples of Phrases	
by the window	in the library
of the train	at the parade
over the roof	on Sunday
the pilot of the airplane	a former resort town

Quick Quiz A

Directions: Underline the phrase in each item. Look for a group of words that cannot stand alone.

1. into the kitchen   cooking
2. sharks   swimming slowly
3. hurricane   turning the path into mud
4. although burned   toast
5. over the rainbow   Dorothy
6. driving   watching the line of cars on the highway
7. into the woods   bears
8. dancer   turning gracefully on one foot
9. under the bed   monster
10. friend   leaving her quick notes

Why Use Phrases?

Phrases are an important part of grammar for several reasons. As you speak and write, you use phrases to:

- Add detail by describing
- Include additional information
- Make your meaning more precise

The following examples show how you can improve your writing by adding phrases. The phrases are underlined.

Adding Phrases to Your Sentences	
Without a Phrase	With a Phrase
The pitcher threw.	The pitcher threw <u>with great speed and skill</u>.
The band marched.	The band marched <u>with loud cheers</u>.
The mayor shook my hand.	The mayor, <u>a popular figure in town</u>, shook my hand.
The sun never shines.	The sun never shines <u>on days when I can enjoy it</u>.

Quick Quiz B

Directions: Add a phrase to each sentence. The phrases are in parentheses ( ). Decide whether to add them to the beginning, middle, or end of the sentence.

1. My father taught school. (for more than thirty years)

    _____

    _____

2. A city is Honolulu. (where I could like to live)

    _____

    _____

3. The rabbit looked happy. (eating carrots)

    _____

    _____

4. Our house stays warm in winter. (sheltered by thick trees)

    _____

    _____

5. She ordered a burger. (loaded with pickles, onions, and ketchup)

    _____

    _____

Quick Quiz C

Directions: Add your own phrase to each sentence. Remember that your phrases should add description. Write the new sentence with the phrase on the line. There are many different phrases you can add. Make sure that your sentence makes sense.

Examples:

Without a phrase: The chicken could not be eaten.

With a phrase: The chicken, completely burned, could not be eaten.

Without a phrase: The chicken could not be eaten.

With a phrase: Burned to a crisp, the chicken could not be eaten.

1.   He grabbed the hand brake.

_____

_____

2.   The chef served corn on the cob.

_____

_____

3.   The lion with strong teeth.

_____

_____

4.   My mother refused.

_____

_____

5.   The plane is flying west.

_____

_____

Appositives

An *appositive* is a noun or a pronoun that renames another noun or pronoun. Appositives are placed directly after the noun or pronoun that they identify. If the appositive is not necessary to the meaning of the sentence, it is set off with commas.

Below are some examples. The appositives are underlined. The noun it renames is in boldface.

Sentence:	The dog sat on the sofa.
Appositive:	a smelly poodle
Sentence with appositive:	The **dog**, <u>a smelly poodle</u>, sat on the sofa.
Sentence:	Larry took the GED.
Appositive:	a battery of six tests
Sentence with appositive:	Larry took the **GED**, <u>a battery of six tests</u>.

Quick Quiz D

Directions: Underline the appositive in each sentence.

1. The GED, the Test of General Educational Development, is recognized around the world.
2. Tasha refused to use the drill, a big and noisy machine.
3. The twins, my cousin's children, are a handful.
4. The clown, also a famous magician, made everyone laugh.
5. The park, located about two miles from my house, has beautiful camp-grounds.

Adding appositives to your writing helps you identify important people, places, and things. This makes your writing clearer. Appositive phrases also let you:

- Get rid of unnecessary words in your sentences
- Write more graceful sentences
- Make your writing more interesting

Quick Quiz E

Directions: Add an appositive phrase to each sentence. The phrases are in parentheses ( ). Add the phrase after the subject. The subject is in **boldface**.

1. Marci gave **Micha** a lovely birthday gift. (her kind neighbor)

    _____

    _____

2. **Lisa** makes beautiful pottery. (my older sister)

    _____

    _____

3. My date took me to a **movie**. (a serious drama about marriage)

    _____

    _____

4. We hoped to win the grand **prize**. (a fabulous cruise)

    _____

    _____

5. The book received a big **prize**. (a bestseller by a new novelist)

    _____

    _____

Quick Quiz F

Directions: Add your own appositive phrase to each sentence. Your appositives should rename the noun. Write the new sentence with the phrase on the line. There are many different appositive phrases you can add. Make sure that your sentence makes sense.

1. My vacation was great.

    _____

    _____

2. The television show was boring.

    _____

    _____

3. Ms. Simmons is retiring this year.

    _____

    _____

Answers to Quick Quizzes

Answers to Quick Quiz A

1. into the kitchen
2. swimming slowly
3. turning the path into mud
4. although burned
5. over the rainbow
6. watching the line of cars on the highway
7. into the woods
8. turning gracefully on one foot
9. under the bed
10. leaving her quick notes

Answers to Quick Quiz B

1. My father taught school for more than thirty years.

   -or-

   For more than thirty years, my father taught school.
2. A city where I could like to live is Honolulu.
3. Eating carrots, the rabbit looked happy.

   -or-

   The rabbit looked happy eating carrots.
4. Sheltered by thick trees, our house stays warm in winter.

   -or-

   Our house stays warm in winter, sheltered by thick trees.
5. She ordered a burger loaded with pickles, onions, and ketchup.

Possible Answers to Quick Quiz C

The phrase is underlined in each sentence.

1. <u>Thinking fast</u>, he grabbed the hand brake.
2. The chef served corn on the cob <u>dripping with butter</u>.
3. The lion with strong teeth <u>crushed his prey</u>.
4. My mother refused <u>to let me go to the dance</u>.
5. The plane <u>carrying my family</u> is flying west.

Answers to Quick Quiz D

(The appositive phrase is underlined in each sentence. The noun it identifies is in boldface.)

1. The **GED**, <u>the Test of General Educational Development</u>, is recognized around the world.

2. Tasha refused to use the **drill**, <u>a big and noisy</u> **machine**.

3. The **twins**, <u>my cousin's children</u>, are a handful.

4. The **clown**, <u>also a famous magician</u>, made everyone laugh.

5. The **park**, <u>located about two miles from my house</u>, has beautiful camp-grounds.

Answers to Quick Quiz E

The appositive phrase is underlined in each sentence. The noun it renames in boldface.

1. Marci gave **Mica**, <u>her kind neighbor</u>, a lovely birthday gift.

2. **Lisa**, <u>my older sister</u>, makes beautiful pottery.

3. My date took me to a **movie,** <u>a serious drama about marriage</u>.

4. We hoped to win the grand **prize**, <u>a fabulous cruise.</u>

5. The **book**, <u>a bestseller by a new novelist</u>, received a big prize.

Possible Answers to Quick Quiz F

The appositive phrase is underlined in each sentence.

1. My vacation, <u>a week in Las Vegas</u>, was great.

2. The television show, <u>a documentary on sea turtles</u>, was boring.

3. Ms. Simmons, <u>my third-grade teacher</u>, is retiring this year.

Grammar Essentials for the Pre-GED Student

Practice Test

Directions: Underline the phrase in each sentence.

1. You will find the test booklets on the desk.
2. For two years, Nick studied for the GED.
3. Becky and her family hike in Mason Park.
4. The dog sat next to its owner.
5. The truck passes by my office daily.
6. The cats chase each other around the house.
7. Jane walked through the parking lot.
8. Rita completed the race despite her injury, a sore knee.
9. Tim gave Patty, his ninety-year-old grandmother, a bouquet of roses.
10. The tree, a majestic old oak, shaded the yard all summer.

Answers

1. You will find the test booklets <u>on the desk</u>.

2. <u>For two years</u>, Nick studied for the GED.

3. Becky and her family hike <u>in Mason Park</u>.

4. The dog sat <u>next to its owner</u>.

5. The truck passes <u>by my office daily</u>.

6. The cats chase each other <u>around the house</u>.

7. Jane walked <u>through the parking lot</u>.

8. Rita completed the race despite her injury, <u>a sore knee.</u>

9. Tim gave Patty, <u>his ninety-year-old grandmother</u>, a bouquet of roses.

10. The tree, <u>a majestic old oak</u>, shaded the yard all summer.

Clauses 9

In this section of the book, you are learning how to build correct sentences. In this chapter, you will learn all about *clauses*. Understanding clauses helps you show how ideas are linked. It also helps you add description to your writing.

What Is a Clause?

A *clause* is a group of words that has its own subject and verb. Remember that a *subject* is the noun or pronoun that does the action. The *verb* is the action word. Here are some examples of clauses. The subjects and verbs are underlined in each one.

Examples of Clauses

The <u>dog</u>	<u>moved</u> fast.
subject	**verb**
<u>I</u>	<u>ran</u> behind the dog.
subject	**verb**
Because the <u>Titanic</u>	<u>sank</u> on its first voyage,
subject	**verb**
Since the <u>GED</u>	<u>includes</u> five different subject tests,
subject	**verb**

There are two kinds of clauses: *independent (main) clauses* and *dependent (subordinate) clauses*. Let's look at each type of clause in detail.

Independent Clauses

An *independent clause* is a complete sentence. This means that it fulfills three requirements:

- It has a subject.
- It has a verb.
- It expresses a complete thought.

You will learn more about sentences in Chapter 10.

The following chart shows some independent clauses divided into their subjects and verbs. The subjects and verbs are underlined.

Examples of Independent Clauses

The <u>car</u>   <u>stalled</u>.
subject   **verb**

The <u>mouse</u>   <u>jumped.</u>
subject   **verb**

<u>Swimming</u>   <u>uses</u> up 200 to 400 calories per hour.
subject   **verb**

<u>Louise</u>   <u>likes</u> oranges, apples, and pears.
subject   **verb**

Quick Quiz A

Directions: Put a check next to the independent clauses. Remember to look for word groups that have a subject, a verb, and express a complete thought.

_____**1.** The GED is 7 1/2 hours long.

_____**2.** Whether you can take the GED.

_____**3.** The GED Science test has 50 questions.

_____**4.** The GED Science test is 80 minutes long.

_____**5.** Nikki took the GED in August.

_____**6.** How much it costs to take the GED.

_____**7.** Passing the GED can help a person in many ways.

_____**8.** Since the GED is given often.

Dependent Clauses

A *dependent (subordinate) clause* is part of a sentence. This means that it cannot stand alone.

It does not express a complete thought. It must be joined with an independent clause.

The following chart shows some dependent clauses. The subjects and verbs are underlined.

Examples of Dependent Clauses

Since <u>dogs</u> <u>come</u> in all shapes and sizes,

    subject verb

When <u>dogs</u> <u>are tamed</u>,

    subject verb

Because working <u>dogs</u> <u>do</u> many jobs,

    subject verb

Do not be fooled by length: An independent clause can be very short, while a dependent clause can be very long!

Quick Quiz B

Directions: Put a check next to the dependent clauses. Remember to look for word groups that have a subject and a verb, but do not express a complete thought.

_____**1.** Each breed of dogs has its own special traits.

_____**2.** Although dogs make great pets,

_____**3.** So that you learn how to take care of your puppy,

_____**4.** Even if you buy a dog from a kennel,

_____**5.** Because dogs hear better than people do,

_____**6.** Dogs have a language all their own.

_____**7.** Most dogs like to have fun.

_____**8.** Some dogs help people.

Linking Dependent and Independent Clauses with Subordinating Conjunctions

A dependent clause often starts with a word that makes the clause unable to stand alone. Look back at the three dependent clauses on the chart. The words used here are *since*, *when*, and *because*. These words are *subordinating conjunctions*, as you learned in Chapter 4.

Remember that a *dependent (subordinate) clause* cannot stand alone. It must be joined with an independent clause. *Subordinating conjunctions* are used to link an independent clause to a dependent clause.

The following chart shows the most common subordinating conjunctions and the relationships they express:

How to Use Subordinating Conjunctions

Subordinating Conjunctions	Relationship	Example
unless, provided that, if, even if	condition	Unless you are on time, we are leaving without you.
because, as, as if	reason	Because the food is good, Jill eats there often.
rather than, than, whether	choice	Whether or not you agree, I intend to take the new job.
though, although, even though, but, unlike	contrast	Although Chris means well, he hurts people's feelings.
where, wherever,	location	Wherever you direct me, I will get lost.
in order that, so, so that, that	result, effect	So that the trip is a success, the guide packs extra maps.
after, as soon, as, before, once, since, until, while, when, whenever	time	After the baby wakes up, Ms. Calla takes her for a walk.

Quick Quiz C

Directions: Join each dependent clause with its independent clause. Place the dependent clause at the beginning or end of the sentence, whichever you think sounds best. Write your answer on the lines provided.

Example: As more spider species evolved. The variety of webs grew.
<u>As more spider species evolved, the variety of webs grew.</u>

1. Even though they have many useful functions. Spiders are scary.

_____

_____

2. All spiders spin silk. But most don't spin webs to catch prey.

_____

_____

3. Unlike spiders that stay in their webs. Jumping spiders have good vision.

_____

_____

4. If you are bitten by a spider. You will have only minor pain.

_____

_____

Answers to Quick Quizzes

Answers to Quick Quiz A

Questions 2, 6, and 8 are not independent clauses because they do not express a complete thought.

Answers to Quick Quiz B

Questions 2, 3, 4, and 5 are dependent clauses because they do not express a complete thought.

Answers to Quick Quiz C

1. Even though they have many useful functions, spiders are scary.
2. All spiders spin silk, but most don't spin webs to catch prey.
3. Unlike spiders that stay in their webs, jumping spiders have good vision.
4. If you are bitten by a spider, you will have only minor pain.

Practice Test

Directions: In the spaces provided, write **D** for dependent clauses or **I** for independent clauses.

1.	Most gems are minerals.
2.	Since minerals are very valuable and rare.
3.	Pearls form the shell of living oysters.
4.	While coral comes from the skeletons of small sea creatures.
5.	Amber is tree resin.
6.	Because diamonds are the hardest minerals.
7.	Scientists make fake gems today.
8.	Although many of these fakes are very beautiful.
9.	Artificial gems are not very costly.
10.	Before you purchase any gems.

Answers

1. I
2. D
3. I
4. D
5. I
6. D
7. I
8. D
9. I
10. D

Sentences | 10

In this chapter, you will use what you learned about phrases and clauses to write complete and correct sentences.

What Is a Sentence?

A sentence is a group of words that expresses a complete idea. To be a sentence, a group of words must:

- Have a *subject* (noun or pronoun)
- Have a *predicate* (verb or verb phrase)
- Express a complete thought

A *sentence* has two parts: A *subject* and a *predicate*. The *subject* includes the noun or pronoun that tells what the sentence is about. The *predicate* includes the verb that describes what the subject is doing. Below are some examples of sentences. The subjects and predicates are underlined in each one.

Examples of Sentences
<u>I</u>   <u>read</u>.
Subject   **Predicate**
<u>Chicago</u>   <u>is called the "Windy City."</u>
Subject   **Predicate**
<u>Radio and television</u>   <u>give us instant information</u>.
Subject   **Predicate**

Quick Quiz A

Directions: Put a check next to the complete sentences. Remember to look for word groups that have a subject, a verb, and express a complete thought.

_____ **1.** What would life be like without inventions?

_____ **2.** The automobile changed our life very much.

_____ **3.** The more Americans bought cars, the more they demanded better roads.

_____ **4.** To travel more quickly.

_____ **5.** In the next century, cars may be powered by electricity.

_____ **6.** Alexander Graham Bell invented the telephone.

_____ **7.** Bell was born in Scotland.

_____ **8.** He taught deaf people.

_____ **9.** His wife was deaf.

_____ **10.** Although everyone today has a telephone.

Independent and dependent clauses can be combined in different ways to form sentences. There are three main kinds of sentences:

- Simple sentences
- Complex sentences
- Compound sentences

Simple Sentences

A *simple sentence* has one independent clause. That means it has one subject and one verb. A simple sentence can also have adjectives and adverbs, and usually does. Here are some examples of simple sentences.

Examples of Simple Sentences
Marconi built the first radio.
Frank Epperson created the Popsicle.
A Swiss engineer invented Velcro.
The Earl of Sandwich invented the sandwich.

Just because it is called the "simple sentence" doesn't mean that it is for children. Using simple sentences can be a powerful way to convey difficult ideas. Because the sentence is short and has just one clause, readers are better able to understand the ideas behind it.

Quick Quiz B

Directions: Put a check next to the simple sentences.

_____   **1.** Clarence Birdseye invented frozen food.

_____   **2.** He got the idea from watching people at the North Pole.

_____   **3.** They froze fish by laying them out on the ice.

_____   **4.** Frozen fish are a good value because they keep their flavor.

_____   **5.** If you catch your own fish, you can freeze them, too.

Quick Quiz C

Directions: Write a simple sentence using the following ideas. Remember to write only one independent clause and no dependent clauses.

1. A favorite invention

_____

_____

2. A beautiful place

_____

_____

3. A special friend

_____

_____

4. A good memory

_____

_____

5. A scary dream

_____

_____

Compound Sentences

A *compound sentence* has two or more independent clauses (simple sentences). The independent clauses can be joined in one of two ways:

- With a coordinating conjunction: *for, and, nor, but, or, yet, so*
- With a semicolon (;)

Just as with a simple sentence, a compound sentence can't have any subordinate clauses. Below are some examples of compound sentences. The independent clauses are underlined. The coordinating conjunction or semicolon is in **boldface**.

Examples of Compound Sentences

<u>Marconi built the first radio</u> **and** <u>he changed the way people get information.</u>
independent clause   *independent clause*

<u>Frank Epperson created the Popsicle</u>, **but** <u>it did not get that name until later</u>.
independent clause   *independent clause*

<u>A Swiss engineer invented Velcro</u>; <u>he got the idea by accident!</u>
independent clause   *independent clause*

<u>The Earl of Sandwich invented the sandwich</u>; <u>he was too busy playing cards to eat a real meal!</u>

independent clause   *independent clause*

Quick Quiz D

Directions: Put a check next to the compound sentences.

_____ **1.** Both the North Pole and the South Pole are cold, but the South Pole is colder.

_____ **2.** The South Pole is a continent.

_____ **3.** It is too cold in the South Pole for plants; people cannot live there either.

_____ **4.** Powerful winds blow across the continent.

_____ **5.** Captain Cook first sailed around the South Pole, but he did not land there.

Directions: Write a compound sentence using the following ideas. Remember to write two independent clauses.

6. cooking

The cooking class I attended was boring and it didn't teach students much on cooking.

7. A good holiday

_____

_____

8. An important goal

_____

_____

9. A personal hero

_____

_____

10. Fierce storms

_____

_____

Complex Sentences

A *complex sentence* has one independent clause and at least one dependent clause. The independent clause is called the "main clause." The dependent clause can be placed before or after the independent clause. These sentences use *subordinating conjunctions* to link ideas. You learned all about subordinating conjunctions in Chapter 4.

Below are some examples of complex sentences. The clause is underlined and labeled. The subordinating conjunction is in **boldface.**

Examples of Complex Sentences

<u>Marc was late</u>   **because**   <u>he overslept</u>.

independent   *subordinating*   *dependent*
clause   *conjunction*   *clause*

Although <u>Marc was late</u>,   <u>we had plenty of food left</u>.

subordinating *dependent*   *independent*
conjunction   *clause*   *clause*

When <u>my mother cooks</u>,   <u>she makes enough food to feed the entire city</u>!

subordinating *dependent*   *independent*
conjunction   *clause*   *clause*

Quick Quiz E

Directions: Put a check next to the complex sentences.

_____ **1.** If you get to the store, please buy me a quart of milk.

_____ **2.** Because the kids are home, we drink a lot of milk.

_____ **3.** After we eat dinner, we can watch television.

_____ **4.** The TV show is funny because the actors do silly things.

_____ **5.** My sister watches a lot of TV even though she should be reading.

_____ **6.** I like action movies.

Which Sentence Types Should You Use?

Should you write simple sentences, compound sentences, or complex sentences? Follow these guidelines as you make your choices:

- Always write complete sentences.
- Give all the information your readers need.
- Put your main point in the independent clause.
- Be sure the ideas you link really *do* go together.
- Check that you have chosen the correct conjunction.
- The more difficult your ideas, the easier and shorter your sentences should be.

Answers to Quick Quizzes

Answers to Quick Quiz A

Only questions 4 and 10 are not sentences.

Answers to Quick Quiz B

Sentences 1, 2, and 3 are simple sentences. Sentences 4 and 5 are not.

Possible Answers to Quick Quiz C

Answers will vary, but here are some possibilities:

1. Television is my favorite invention.
2. The Grand Canyon is a beautiful place.
3. Tricia is my best friend.
4. My wedding day was a beautiful day.
5. I dreamed of monsters last night.

Answers to Quick Quiz D

Sentences 1, 3, and 5 are compound sentences. Sentences 2 and 4 are simple sentences.

Since the answers to 6–10 will vary, here are some possible answers:

6. Felice is a good cook, but Richie is a fussy eater.
7. On Thanksgiving we play football and we have a big meal.
8. Dion wants to pass his GED so he can get a better job.
9. My father is my hero; he overcame great hardship.
10. The hurricane smashed the barn, yet it spared the house.

Answers to Quick Quiz E

Sentences 1–5 are complex sentences; sentence 6 is a simple sentence.

Practice Test

Directions: Label each sentence simple, compound, or complex. Write your answer in the space provided for you.

_____ **1.** Blood delivers chemicals to all your organs and it carts away the waste.

_____ **2.** Although blood is a lifesaver, it can also spread poisons in your body.

_____ **3.** Germs can get into your bloodstream.

_____ **4.** Red blood cells pick up oxygen so your cells are nourished.

_____ **5.** White blood cells are larger than red blood cells.

_____ **6.** If you donate blood, you can help save lives.

_____ **7.** Even though some people think donating blood hurts, the process is painless.

_____ **8.** You can feel your pulse in your neck.

_____ **9.** Scientists cannot make artificial blood, yet they are working very hard on it.

_____ **10.** If your blood gets too thick, you might have a heart attack.

_____ **11.** It takes just five minutes to donate blood.

_____ **12.** Type O is the most common blood; Type A is the next most common type.

Answers

1. compound sentence
2. complex sentence
3. simple sentence
4. compound sentence
5. simple sentence
6. complex sentence
7. complex sentence
8. simple sentence
9. compound sentence
10. complex sentence
11. simple sentence
12. compound sentence

Common Grammar Problems

Correcting Sentence Errors | 11

The two most common sentence errors are *fragments* and *run-ons*. In this chapter, you will learn how to correct these sentence errors. This will help you express yourself in writing with confidence.

What Is a Fragment?

As you learned in Chapter 10, a sentence is a group of words that expresses a complete idea. Every complete sentence has a *subject* (noun or pronoun), a *predicate* (verb or verb phrase), and expresses a complete thought.

A *fragment* is a group of words that does not express a complete thought. Fragments are created when:

- A subject is missing.

- A verb is missing.

- Both a subject and verb are missing.

- The word group does not express a complete thought.

Examples of Fragments

no subject:

Have wings that do not help in flying.   (*What* has wings?)

Can swim almost thirty miles an hour.   (*Who* or *what* can swim?)

no verb:

The penguins in the South Pole.   (*Do* what?)

The first NASA astronauts.   (*Did* what?)

no subject or verb:

Thousands of miles every year.

In the box under the bed.

not a complete thought:

Because the pyramids fascinate people.

If you visit the pyramids.

Don't be fooled by a capital letter at the beginning of a word group or a period at the end. Just because a group of words starts with a capital letter and ends with a period does not make it a sentence.

Quick Quiz A

Directions: Put a check next to the fragments.

_____ **1.** Have become polluted.

_____ **2.** Is very unhealthy for people, plants, and animals.

_____ **3.** Have dumped sewage into rivers, causing pollution.

_____ **4.** A council of advisors to the United States.

_____ **5.** Some big factories in the area.

_____ **6.** In the woods late into the night.

_____ **7.** Traveling slowly by foot.

_____ **8.** Because people assumed rivers would carry away the waste.

_____ **9.** If some factories pour hot water into a river.

_____ **10.** Rivers can handle some waste bacteria.

Correcting Fragments

To correct a fragment, all you have to do is add the missing parts. In the chart below, you'll see that the added parts are underlined.

Correcting Fragments	
Fragment	Sentence
Have wings that do not help in flying.	Penguins have wings that do not help in flying.
Can swim almost thirty. miles an hour.	Polar bears can swim almost thirty miles an hour.
The penguins in the South Pole.	The penguins in the South Pole live in packs.
The first NASA astronauts.	The first NASA astronauts became famous.
Thousands of miles every year.	The salesman travels thousands of miles every year.
If you visit the pyramids.	If you visit the pyramids, bring me a picture!

Quick Quiz B

Directions: Correct each fragment by adding the missing information. When you add the missing information, you'll create a complete sentence.

1. Have become polluted.

    _____

    _____

2. Is very unhealthy for people, plants, and animals.

    _____

    _____

3. Have dumped sewage into rivers, causing pollution.

    _____

    _____

4. Some big factories in the area.

    _____

    _____

5. Because people assumed rivers would carry away the waste

    _____

    _____

6. If some factories pour hot water into a river

    _____

    _____

7. When water vapor rises into the air.

    _____

    _____

8. Falls from clouds to the earth.

    _____

    _____

9. Melting snow and rain.

    _____

    _____

10. As I was rowing slowly down the river.

    _____

    _____

What Is a Run-on Sentence?

A *run-on sentence* is two *incorrectly* joined independent clauses. Run-ons are created when:

- Two sentences are run together without any punctuation.

- A comma (,) is used instead of a semicolon (;), colon (:), or coordinating conjunction (*and, but, for, nor, or, so, yet*) to join two complete sentences.

Examples of Run-on Sentences

Sentences run together:

Day ended at dusk drivers pulled their wagons into a circle.

The people put up tents oxen grazed in the circle.

Sentences joined incorrectly:

Day ended at dusk drivers, pulled their wagons into a circle.

The people put up tents, oxen grazed in the circle.

Do not assume that run-ons are long. Some can be quite short, in fact. Here are two examples:

Run-On	*Correct Sentences*
She talked he listened.	She talked, and he listened.
I read my husband watched TV.	I read while my husband watched TV.

Quick Quiz C

Directions: Put a check next to the run-on sentences.

_____ **1.** The first pioneers moved west in the 1760s; the second group came eighty years later.

_____ **2.** Daniel Boone connected trails he helped many pioneers.

_____ **3.** The Wilderness Road was the best route through the mountains over 200,000 pioneers traveled on it.

_____ **4.** Some pioneers traveled by the Ohio River it was an easier route than the mountains.

_____ **5.** Later the pioneers took the boats apart they used the wood for their houses.

_____ **6.** Settlers built log cabins they had to cut all the logs by hand.

_____ **7.** Pioneers ate a lot of corn because it was easy to grow.

_____ **8.** Families ate cornbread they fed the leftovers to the hogs.

_____ **9.** Some Americans headed west to find gold; others hoped for better health in the mild California climate.

_____ **10.** Families filled their wagons with supplies they had to carry a lot of things.

Correcting Run-Ons

There are four ways to correct a run-on:

1. **Make two sentences**

Run-on	*Correct Sentence*
Daniel Boone connected trails	Daniel Boone connected trails.
he helped many pioneers.	He helped many pioneers.

2. **Add a coordinating conjunction (and, nor, but, or, for, yet, so) to create a compound sentence.**

Run-on	*Correct Sentence*
Daniel Boone connected trails	Daniel Boone connected trails, so
he helped many pioneers.	he helped many pioneers.

3. **Add a subordinating conjunction to create a complex sentence.**

Run-on	*Correct Sentence*
Daniel Boone connected trails	Because Daniel Boone connected trails,
he helped many pioneers.	he helped many pioneers.

4. **Use a semicolon to create a compound sentence.**

Run-on	*Correct Sentence*
Daniel Boone connected trails	Daniel Boone connected trails;
he helped many pioneers.	he helped many pioneers.

Quick Quiz D

Directions: Correct each run-on. Use one of the four methods of correcting run-on sentences.

1. The Wilderness Road was the best route through the mountains over 200,000 pioneers traveled on it.

   _____

   _____

2. Some pioneers traveled by the Ohio River it was an easier route than the mountains.

   _____

   _____

3. Later the pioneers took the boats apart they used the wood for their houses.

   _____

   _____

4. Settlers built log cabins they had to cut all the logs by hand.

   _____

   _____

5. Families ate cornbread they fed the leftovers to the hogs.

   _____

   _____

6. Families filled their wagons with supplies they had to carry a lot of things.

   _____

   _____

Answers to Quick Quizzes

Answers to Quick Quiz A

Questions 1–9 are fragments. Only question 10 is a complete sentence.

Possible Answers to Quick Quiz B

Sentences will vary. Here are some sample answers:

1. Many rivers have become polluted.
2. Pollution is very unhealthy for people, plants, and animals.
3. Factories have dumped sewage into rivers, causing pollution.
4. Some big factories in the area are cleaning up pollution.
5. Because people assumed rivers would carry away the waste, they did not worry about pollution.
6. If some factories pour hot water into a river, plants and animals often die.
7. When water vapor rises into the air, it cools and turns into drops of water.
8. Rain falls from clouds to the earth.
9. Melting snow and rain clog our streets.
10. As I was rowing slowly down the river, I saw beautiful houses.

Answers to Quick Quiz C

Questions 2, 3, 4, 5, 6, 8, and 10 are run-on sentences. Items 1, 7, and 9 are complete sentences.

Possible Answers to Quick Quiz D

Sentences will vary. Here are some sample answers:

1. The Wilderness Road was the best route through the mountains, so over 200,000 pioneers traveled on it.
2. Some pioneers traveled by the Ohio River because it was an easier route than the mountains.
3. Later the pioneers took the boats apart, and they used the wood for their houses.
4. Settlers built log cabins, but they had to cut all the logs by hand.
5. Families ate cornbread, and they fed the leftovers to the hogs.
6. Families filled their wagons with supplies; they had to carry a lot of things.

Practice Test

Directions: Write **FRAG** if the sentence is a fragment. Write **RO** if the sentence is a run-on. Write **C** if the sentence is correct. Next, on a separate sheet of paper, correct all the fragments and run-ons.

_____ **1.** Went camping last week.

_____ **2.** We left Friday we returned Sunday.

_____ **3.** A bear wandered into the campground I was not scared.

_____ **4.** Wanted some food.

_____ **5.** We also saw squirrels, but they left us alone.

_____ **6.** My old friend Brett from Michigan.

_____ **7.** We met on the job we have been friends for more than 10 years.

_____ **8.** As we sat around the campfire singing, I felt very happy.

_____ **9.** Although I cannot sing well.

_____ **10.** We packed up the gear, we carefully put out the campfire.

Answers

1. FRAG
2. RO
3. RO
4. FRAG
5. C
6. FRAG
7. RO
8. C
9. FRAG
10. RO

Possible Answers

1. We went camping last week.
2. We left Friday, and we returned Sunday.
3. A bear wandered into the campground, but I was not scared.
4. The bear wanted some food.
6. My old friend Brett from Michigan met us there.
7. We met on the job; we have been friends for more than 10 years.
9. Although I cannot sing well, no one makes fun of me.
10. Before we packed up the gear, we carefully put out the campfire.

Agreement of Subject and Verb 12

You know that every sentence needs a subject and a verb—but not just any subject and verb! The subject and verb must fit together correctly. That is what this chapter will teach you.

What Is Agreement?

Agreement means that parts of the sentence match. The subject and verb must be in the same number. In grammar, *number* means "singular" or "plural." Otherwise, the sentence does not sound right. Even more serious, the sentence may not correctly convey your meaning.

How Can I Tell Singular from Plural?

Before you can make sentence parts agree, you have to be sure you can form singular and plural nouns and verbs. Follow these guidelines.

Nouns
Most nouns form the plural by adding *-s* or *-es*. Here are some examples:

Singular Nouns	Plural Nouns
book	books
carrot	carrots
car	cars

As you learned in Chapter 1, other nouns form irregular plurals. These include *child/children*, *foot/feet*, and *sheep/sheep*, for example.

Verbs

Verbs do not follow the same rule as nouns. Instead, the third-person singular form of most verbs ends in *-s* or *-es*. The following chart can help you remember how to use verbs correctly. It contains examples of regular verbs.

Present-Tense Verbs		
I walk	I swim	I read
you walk	you swim	you read
we walk	we swim	we read
they walk	they swim	they read
he, she, it walk*s*	he, she, it swim*s*	he, she, it read*s*

When used as a helping verb, *be*, *do*, and *have* change form so that they agree with a third-person singular subject. The main verb does not add *-s*.

Incorrect: Does the store <u>opens</u> at 10:00?

Correct: Does the store <u>open</u> at 10:00?

Quick Quiz A

Directions: Circle the *plural noun* in each pair.

1. opera   operas
2. paintings   painting
3. fable   fables
4. rhymes   rhyme
5. pear   pears
6. child   children

Quick Quiz B

Directions: Circle the *singular verb* in each pair.

1. is   are
2. was   were
3. leap   leaps
4. shatters shatter
5. fall   falls
6. drips   drip

Rules for Agreement of Subject and Verb

Rule #1: A singular subject takes a singular verb.

Remember that "singular" means *one*. Below are some examples of a singular subject taking a singular verb. The subjects and verbs are underlined and labeled.

The <u>basketball player</u> <u>is</u> very good.
       singular   **singular**
       subject   **verb**

My <u>sister</u> <u>was</u> late again.
singular **singular**
subject   **verb**

<u>Mary</u> <u>belongs</u> to a bowling league.
singular **singular**
subject   **verb**

The <u>King</u> <u>gives</u> gifts to his friends.
singular **singular**
subject   **verb**

Singular subjects connected by *either/or, neither/nor,* and *not only/but also* require a singular verb. That's because the connecting words show that you are choosing only one item. Below is an example. The subjects and verbs are underlined and labeled.

<u>Either my sister or my brother</u> <u>is</u> going to sit here.
       singular   **singular**
       subject   **verb**

Only <u>one</u> person is going to sit here: my sister or my brother. Therefore, the subject is singular. The singular subject ("sister" or "brother") matches the singular verb ("is").

Quick Quiz C

Directions: Choose the correct verb to complete each sentence.

1. Gary always (brings, bring) the soda to the party.

2. Either Adrienne or Louise (is, are) buying the pizza.

3. My mother (make, makes) rice and peas.

4. The food (disappears, disappear) fast!

5. The music (were, was) lively.

6. The party (was, were) a big success.

7. My brother (are, is) very hard working.

8. I (likes, like) to travel.

9. Hester (packs, pack) light so she doesn't have to carry much.

10. My friend (carry, carries) far too much.

Collective Nouns

Collective nouns are singular in form but plural in sense. Here are some examples of collective nouns:

Collective Nouns			
audience	assembly	class	faculty
committee	crowd	family	jury
flock	herd	team	crew

Below are some examples of collective nouns taking a singular verb. The subjects and verbs are underlined and labeled.

The <u>jury</u> <u>is</u> out.
singular singular
 subject   verb

The <u>team</u> <u>wins</u> every game.
singular singular
 subject verb

Rule #2: A plural subject takes a plural verb

"Plural" means *more than one*. Below are some examples of a plural subject taking a plural verb. The subjects and verbs are underlined and labeled.

<u>Stephen and Shelby</u> <u>are</u> going to the movies.

plural   **plural**
subject   **verb**

<u>My friends</u>   <u>buy</u> fresh fruit at the market.

plural   **plural**
subject   **verb**

<u>Mary and Tina</u>   <u>belong</u> to a bowling league.

pluralplural
subject   **verb**

The <u>King and Queen</u> <u>give</u> gifts to their friends.

plural   **plural**
subject   **verb**

Think of the conjunction "and" as a plus sign. Whether the parts of the subject joined by "and" are singular or plural (or both), they all add up to a plural subject and so require a plural verb.

If the subject is made up of two or more nouns or pronouns connected by *or, nor, not only,* or *but also,* the verb agrees with the noun closer to the pronoun. Below are some examples. The subjects and verbs are underlined and labeled.

Either the dog or the <u>cats</u> <u>are</u> howling.
The plural subject "cats" agrees with the plural verb "are."

Neither the cats nor the <u>dog</u> <u>is</u> howling.
The singular subject "dog" agrees with the singular verb "is."

Quick Quiz D

Directions: Choose the correct verb to complete each sentence.

1. The company's workers (is, are) going to a picnic.
2. The packages (arrive, arrives) late.
3. The vegetables (was, were) overcooked.
4. The cooks (comes, come) in late.
5. Either the plumber or the tree trimmers (are, is) coming over today.
6. Either the tree trimmers or the plumber (are, is) coming over today.
7. Heavy rain and high winds (is, are) wrecking our vacation.
8. The tractors (moves, move) the dirt from the area.
9. The plows (remove, removes) the snow.
10. My friends (is, are) coming over later.

Answers to Quick Quizzes

Answers to Quick Quiz A

1. operas
2. paintings
3. fables
4. rhymes
5. pears
6. children

Answers to Quick Quiz B

1. is
2. was
3. leaps
4. shatters
5. falls
6. drips

Answers to Quick Quiz C

1. brings
2. is
3. makes
4. disappears
5. was
6. was
7. is
8. like
9. packs
10. carries

Answers to Quick Quiz D

1. are
2. arrive
3. were
4. come
5. are
6. is
7. are
8. move
9. remove
10. are

Practice Test

Directions: First, read the subject. Second, choose the verb that agrees with the subject and underline it. Last, write the rule that applies. The first one is done for you.

	Subject	**Verb**	**Rule**
1.	boys	(is/<u>are</u>)	plural subject = plural verb
2.	laborers	(were/was)	_____
3.	employee	(has/have)	_____
4.	students	(want/wants)	_____
5.	wives	(need/needs)	_____
6.	husband	(buy/buys)	_____
7.	children	(give/gives)	_____
8.	pet	(shed/sheds)	_____
9.	model	(wear/wears)	_____
10.	trains	(go/goes)	_____

Directions: Choose the correct verb to complete each sentence.

11. Many people (has, have) taken the GED.

12. They (was, were) happy to get a high school diploma.

13. Exercise (is, are) good for you.

14. However, I still (does, do) not like to exercise.

15. Pat (prefer, prefers) to read.

16. Nanci (gets, get) her exercise dancing.

17. My friends (jog, jogs) for fun.

18. Tom (jogs, jog) fast, but Greg (run, runs) more slowly.

19. They (is, are) healthy because of their efforts.

20. Marci still (like, likes) to sit around and watch TV!

Answers

	Subject	Verb	Rule
1.	boys	(is/<u>are</u>)	plural subject = plural verb
2.	laborers	were	plural subject = plural verb
3.	employee	has	singular subject = singular verb
4.	students	want	plural subject = plural verb
5.	wives	need	plural subject = plural verb
6.	husband	buys	singular subject = singular verb
7.	children	give	plural subject = plural verb
8.	pet	sheds	singular subject = singular verb
9.	model	wears	singular subject = singular verb
10.	trains	go	plural subject = plural verb

11.	have
12.	were
13.	is
14.	do
15.	prefers
16.	gets
17.	jog
18.	jogs, runs
19.	are
20.	likes

Dangling and Misplaced Modifiers | 13

Modifiers are words that describe. There are two kinds of modifiers: Adjectives and adverbs. You learned all about adjectives in Chapter 5. You learned all about adverbs in Chapter 6. Errors occur when adjectives and adverbs are misused. Two of the most common errors are *dangling modifiers* and *misplaced modifiers*. This chapter shows you how to avoid these grammatical errors.

What Are Dangling Modifiers?

What is wrong with the following sentence?

Walking down the stairs, the clock struck ten.

As it's written, the sentence states that the clock was walking down the stairs. We know that clocks cannot walk. The error occurs because the phrase "walking down the stairs" has nothing to modify or describe. A *dangling modifier* is a word or phrase that describes something that has been left out of the sentence.

Remember that a *modifier* is a word or phrase that gives more information about the subject, verb, or object in a clause. A modifier is said to "dangle" when the word it modifies is not actually in the sentence. "Walking down the stairs" is a dangling modifier because it cannot be attached to any word in the sentence.

Dangling modifiers confuse your readers. They make your meaning unclear. They may also create humor when you are not trying to be funny.

Correcting Dangling Modifiers

Since the basic problem with a dangling modifier is a lack of connection, you must provide a noun or pronoun to which the dangling modifier can be linked.

Rewrite the main clause so the subject or object can be modified by the phrase. There are different ways that you can rewrite the sentence, as long as it makes sense. Here are some examples:

Dangling: Giving a party, several balloons were blown up.
Correct: Giving a party, they blew up several balloons.
(Now, <u>they</u> are the ones blowing up the balloons.)

Dangling: Do not play on the swing without being fully assembled.
Correct: You should not play on the swing unless it is fully assembled.
(Now, <u>you</u> are the one who should not play on the swing unless <u>it</u> is assembled.)

Dangling: Flying over Kansas, the cars and farms looked like toys.
Correct: As we flew over Kansas, the cars and farms looked like toys.
(Now, <u>we</u> are the ones flying over Kansas.)

Dangling: After studying, the GED was a breeze.
Correct: After Jack studied, the GED was a breeze.
(Now, <u>Jack</u> is the person doing the studying.)

Quick Quiz A

Directions: Explain the dangling modifier in each sentence.

1. Stored under the bed for 20 years, the owner of the stamps decided to sell them.

    _____

    _____

2. Important facts might be revealed when leaving.

    _____

    _____

3. While driving into town, a crash was seen.

    _____

    _____

4. While eating lunch, a bug slipped into her soup.

    _____

    _____

5. Sailing up the river, the New York skyline was seen.

    _____

    _____

Quick Quiz B

Directions: Rewrite each of the following sentences to correct the dangling modifier.

1. Stored under the bed for 20 years, the owner of the stamps decided to sell them.

   _____

   _____

2. Important facts might be revealed when leaving.

   _____

   _____

3. While driving into town, a crash was seen.

   _____

   _____

4. While eating lunch, a bug slipped into her soup.

   _____

   _____

5. Sailing up the river, the New York skyline was seen.

   _____

   _____

What Are Misplaced Modifiers?

What is wrong with the following sentence?

We bought a kitten for my sister we call Fluffy.

As this sentence is written, it means that the sister, not the kitten, is called Fluffy. That's because the modifier "we call Fluffy" is in the wrong place in the sentence. This grammar error is called a *misplaced modifier*. A *misplaced modifier* is a phrase, clause, or word placed too far from the word or words it modifies (describes).

Correcting Misplaced Modifiers

To correct a misplaced modifier, move the modifier as close as possible to the word or phrase it describes. Here is how the previous incorrect sentence should read:

We bought a kitten we call Fluffy for my sister.

Below are some more examples.

Misplaced: The student was referred to a tutor with learning disabilities.

Correct: The student with learning disabilities was referred to a tutor.

(Now, <u>the student</u> rather than the tutor has the learning disabilities.)

Misplaced: Danielle found a sweater in the car that doesn't belong to her.

Correct: Danielle found a sweater that doesn't belong to her in the car.

(Now, <u>the sweater</u> doesn't belong to Danielle, not the car.)

Misplaced: A bracelet was reported stolen by the police yesterday.

Correct: The police reported that a bracelet was stolen yesterday.

(Now, <u>the police</u> reported the bracelet stolen—rather than stealing it.)

Quick Quiz C

Directions: Explain why the modifier in each sentence is misplaced.

1.   The golfer made a hole-in-one with the green shirt.

_____

_____

2.   The house was rebuilt by the people destroyed by the fire.

_____

_____

3.   We saw many beautiful homes driving through the South.

_____

_____

4.   Jen bought a ring from a jeweler with diamonds.

_____

_____

5.   We need someone to take care of a dog who does not smoke or drink.

_____

_____

Quick Quiz D

Directions: Rewrite each of the following sentences to correct the misplaced modifier.

1.   The golfer made a hole-in-one with the green shirt.

_____

_____

2.   The house was rebuilt by the people destroyed by the fire.

_____

_____

3.   We saw many beautiful homes driving through the South.

_____

_____

4.   Jen bought a ring from a jeweler with diamonds.

_____

_____

5.   We need someone to take care of a dog who does not smoke or drink.

_____

_____

Answers to Quick Quizzes

Answers to Quick Quiz A

1. This sentence states that the owner of the stamps was stored under the bed for 20 years.

2. According to this sentence, the facts are leaving.

3. This sentence states that the crash is doing the driving.

4. According to this sentence, the bug is eating lunch.

5. This sentence states that the New York skyline is sailing up the river.

Possible Answers to Quick Quiz B

Answers will vary. Here are some possible ways to correct each dangling modifier:

1. The owner decided to sell the stamps, which had been stored under the bed for 20 years.

2. You might reveal important facts when you leave. -or-

   Important facts might be revealed when you leave.

3. While we were driving into town, we saw a crash. -or-

   While driving into town, we saw a crash.

4. While Kri was eating lunch, a bug slipped into her soup.

5. As we sailed up the river, we saw the New York skyline. -or-

   Sailing up the river, we saw the New York skyline.

Answers to Quick Quiz C

1. This sentence states that the hole in one, not the golfer, is wearing a green shirt.

2. According to this sentence, the people (not the house) were destroyed in the fire.

3. This sentence states that the homes, not the people, were driving through the South.

4. According to this sentence, the jeweler (not the ring) had diamonds.

5. This sentence states that the dog does not drink or smoke.

Answers to Quick Quiz D

1. The golfer with the green shirt made a hole-in-one.
2. The house destroyed by the fire was rebuilt by the people.
3. Driving through the South, we saw many beautiful homes.
4. Jen bought a ring with diamonds from a jeweler.
5. We need someone who does not smoke or drink to take care of a dog.

Practice Test

Directions: Correct the following dangling modifiers.

1.   Absorbed in the book, the time passed quickly.

2.   Driving through the desert at night, the moon looked huge.

3.   Although tired of running, it was good to reach their goal.

4.   While at dinner, a glass of water fell into her lap.

5.   To succeed on the GED, studying can't be avoided.

Directions: Correct the following misplaced modifiers.

6.   Smashed beyond repair, Bob saw his watch on the ground.

7.   Please take time to look over the brochure that is enclosed with your family.

8.   The writer read from his new book wearing glasses.

9.   After selling all the merchandise, the profit made was almost fifty dollars.

10.   Doing new dances, his records were bought by teenagers.

Answers

Answers will vary. Here are some possible ways to correct each dangling modifier:

1. Because Ian was absorbed in the book, the time passed quickly.
2. As Leroy was driving through the desert at night, the moon looked huge.
3. Although they were tired of running, it was good to reach their goal.
4. While she was at dinner, a glass of water fell into her lap.
5. To succeed on the GED, you can't avoid studying.

Answers

6. Bob saw his watch smashed beyond repair on the ground.
7. Please take time to look over the enclosed brochure with your family.
8. Wearing glasses, the writer read from his new book.
9. After selling all the merchandise, I made a profit of almost fifty dollars.
10. His records were bought by teenagers doing new dances.

Correcting Double Negatives | 14

What Is a Double Negative?

A *double negative* is a sentence that contains two negative describing words. The following chart shows the most common negative words.

Negative Words	
no	never
not	none
nothing	hardly
scarcely	barely
n't (as used in a contraction such as *didn't, couldn't, wouldn't*)	

Look back at the chart. See how many negative words begin with "N." These include *no, not, nothing, never, none.* Think of the letter "N" to help you remember negative words.

Below are some sentences with double negatives. The double negative word in each example is underlined.

Sentences with Double Negatives

We did <u>not</u> have <u>no</u> money.

negative word	**negative word**

He could<u>n't</u> do <u>nothing</u>.

negative word	**negative word**

I do<u>n't</u> want <u>no</u> more salad.

negative word	**negative word**

Correcting Double Negatives

To correct a double negative, take out one of the negative words. Add a pronoun or a single negative word.

Double negative: We did <u>not</u> have <u>no</u> money.
Correct: We did <u>not</u> have <u>any</u> money.
           negative   **pronoun**
              word

-or-

We had <u>no</u> money.
     negative
      word

Double negative: He could<u>n't</u> do <u>nothing</u>.
Correct: He could<u>n't</u> do <u>anything</u>.
           negative   **pronoun**
              word

-or-

He did <u>nothing</u>.
     negative
      word

Quick Quiz A

Directions: Circle the two negative words in each sentence. Write your answers on the lines provided.

1. I don't want no more salad.

   _____ _____

2. I didn't have no job.

   _____ _____

3. I'm so full that I can't eat nothing.

   _____ _____

4. They couldn't hardly finish their meal on time.

   _____ _____

5. She has never done nothing to hurt me.

   _____ _____

6. It was so dark that we couldn't read none of the signs.

   _____ _____

7. Don't smoke nowhere near me!

   _____ _____

8. No one at the party ate none of the snacks.

   _____ _____

9. Nobody said nothing to me about a study session.

   _____ _____

10. The family didn't get nothing in the will.

    _____ _____

Quick Quiz B

Directions: Rewrite each sentence to correct the double negative.

1.   I don't want no more salad.

   _____

   _____

2.   I didn't have no job.

   _____

   _____

3.   I'm so full that I can't eat nothing.

   _____

   _____

4.   They couldn't hardly finish their meal on time.

   _____

   _____

5.   She has never done nothing to hurt me.

   _____

   _____

6.   It was so dark that we couldn't read none of the signs.

   _____

   _____

7.   Don't smoke nowhere near me!

   _____

   _____

8.   No one at the party ate none of the snacks.

   _____

   _____

9.   Nobody said nothing to me about a study session.

   _____

   _____

10.   The family didn't get nothing in the will.

   _____

   _____

Answers to Quick Quizzes

Answers to Quick Quiz A

1. don't, no
2. didn't, no
3. can't, nothing
4. couldn't, hardly
5. never, nothing
6. couldn't, none
7. Don't, nowhere
8. No, none
9. Nobody, nothing
10. didn't, nothing

Possible Answers to Quick Quiz B

1. I don't want any more salad.
2. I didn't have a job.
3. I'm so full that I can't eat anything.
4. They could hardly finish their meal on time.
5. She has never done anything to hurt me.
6. It was so dark that we couldn't read any of the signs.
7. Don't smoke anywhere near me!
8. No one at the party ate any of the snacks.
9. Nobody said anything to me about a study session.
10. The family didn't get anything in the will.

Practice Test

Directions: Circle the negative word in each line.

1.	anyone	no
2.	someone	nothing
3.	something	didn't
4.	can't	any
5.	nothing	some
6.	scarcely	anything
7.	all	never
8.	any	none
9.	others	hardly
10.	barely	several

Directions: Rewrite each sentence to correct the double negative.

11. We didn't scarcely know him.

_____

_____

12. I couldn't hardly see in the fog.

_____

_____

13. She wasn't barely asleep when the phone rang.

_____

_____

14. There wasn't but one movie.

_____

_____

15. I don't want to see no one.

_____

_____

16. She doesn't like me no more.

_____

_____

17.   My grandfather can't hardly read the small print.

_____

_____

18.   She didn't have no time for me.

_____

_____

19.   Nora couldn't scarcely catch her breath.

_____

_____

20.   We haven't traveled nowhere in a long time.

_____

_____

Answers

1. no
2. nothing
3. didn't
4. can't
5. nothing
6. scarcely
7. never
8. none
9. hardly
10. barely

Possible Answers

11. We scarcely know him.
12. I could hardly see in the fog.
13. She was barely asleep when the phone rang.
14. There was but one movie. –or- There was only one movie.
15. I don't want to see anyone.
16. She doesn't like me any more.
17. My grandfather can hardly read the small print.
18. She didn't have any time for me.
19. Nora could scarcely catch her breath.
20. We haven't traveled anywhere in a long time.

Mechanics

Using Commas Correctly | 15

Using the correct punctuation helps your readers understand your ideas more clearly. Commas help us read numbers and dates. Commas also tell us how to read and understand sentences because they tell us where to pause. Here are the rules for using commas correctly.

Use Commas with Dates and Numbers

- Use a comma between the day of the month and the year. Here are some examples:

  December 25, 2003   March 16, 1989

  July 20, 1969   May 1, 2004

- Use commas to show thousands, millions, and so on. Put a comma after every three numbers from the right. Here are some examples:

1,500	10,088	1,345,901
103,000	1,000,000	192,571

Quick Quiz A

Directions: Add commas as needed.

1. January 1 2004
2. April 4 1951
3. June 17 2003
4. August 31 2004
5. 3000
6. 240000
7. 51000
8. 412567

Use Commas with Addresses

Use a comma to separate the parts of an address. Put commas between the street, town, and state. Do not put a comma between the state and the zip code. Here are some examples:

We are visiting <u>671 Plitt Avenue</u>, <u>King City</u>, <u>California</u> 93930
street　　　town　　state　zip code

She lives at <u>38 Longacre Drive</u>, <u>Bisbee</u>, <u>Arizona</u> 85603
street　　　town　state　zip code

I was born at <u>81A Polly Ann Terrace</u>, <u>Beacon Falls</u>, <u>Connecticut</u> 06403
street　　　town　　　state　zip code

Quick Quiz B

Directions: Add commas as needed.

1. We sent the package to 74 Adams Street Arcadia Florida 34266.
2. The party is being held at 190 Clark Road Ammon Idaho 83401.
3. There is an open house at 17 Main Street Addison Illinois 60101.
4. My sister just moved to 91-82 Fifth Boulevard Muncie Indiana 47302.
5. Wait until you see the house at 10196 Willowbrook Avenue Mayfield Kentucky 42066.
6. My father is staying at 353 Lexington Street Lewison Maine 04240.

Use Commas in Letters

- Use a comma after the greeting of an informal letter. Here are some examples:

Dear Kathy,　　Dear Victoria,

Dear Antoine,　　Dear Anneka,

- Use a comma at the close of any letter. Here are some examples:

Yours truly,　　Sincerely,

Thank you,　　Very truly yours,

Quick Quiz C

Directions: Add commas as needed. Write your answers on the lines provided for you.

---

(1) Dear Aunt Felice

Thank you for the loan of **(2)** $1000. I found a good used car. It costs only **(3)** $5000. I have saved **(4)** $4000 so now I have enough to buy the car. It will make it much easier for me to get to work. Thank you again.

(5) Very truly yours

Natalya

---

1. _____

2. _____

3. _____

4. _____

5. _____

Use a Comma Between Parts of a Compound Sentence

Use a comma to separate parts of a compound sentence. As you learned in Chapter 10, a *compound sentence* has two or more independent clauses (simple sentences). The independent clauses can be joined with a coordinating conjunction or with a semicolon (;). This comma rule applies to compound sentences whose parts are joined with a coordinating conjunction.

Use the comma before the coordinating conjunction. Remember: The coordinating conjunctions are *and, but, or, nor, for, so,* and *yet.* The coordinating conjunction is underlined in the following examples.

I went to the movies last weekend, <u>but</u> the show was sold out.

Barry visited the pyramids in Egypt, <u>for</u> he has always been interested in them.

I paid a lot of money for the refrigerator, <u>so</u> I expected it to last a long time.

Quick Quiz D

Directions: Add commas as needed.

1. The Moon constantly circles Earth and Earth constantly circles the Sun.
2. Earth spins very fast but we do not ever feel it.
3. Amy studies the solar system for she wants to be an astronaut.
4. She will take a lot of science in school so she is well prepared.
5. This summer, she is going to space camp or she will take some extra classes.
6. Amy knows this will be difficult yet she is determined to succeed.

Use a Comma to Set off a Direct Quotation

A *direct quotation* is a speaker's exact words. A direct quotation starts and ends with quotation marks. Here are some examples:

speaker at the beginning:	Luc said, "It is warm enough to walk to work."
speaker at the end:	"It is warm enough to walk to work," Luc said.
speaker in the middle:	"It is warm enough," Luc said, "to walk to work."

Quick Quiz E

Directions: Add commas as needed.

1. "I will be late tonight because of the party" Ruth said.
2. Ruth said "I will be late tonight because of the party."
3. "I will be late tonight" Ruth said "because of the party."
4. "Don't forget that I have to take Ralph to the doctor" Robbie said.
5. Robbie said "Don't forget that I have to take Ralph to the doctor."
6. "Don't forget" Robbie said "that I have to take Ralph to the doctor."

Use a Comma with a List

Use a comma between the items in a list. Here are some examples:

> The colors in a rainbow are red, orange, yellow, green, blue, indigo, and violet.

> Planets, their moons, and asteroids circle the Sun.

> The travelers ironed their clothing, folded it neatly, and packed their bags.

Quick Quiz F

Directions: Add commas as needed.

1. Earth's crust contains nickel iron and rock.
2. Venus is so hot that lead tin and zinc would melt there in a flash.
3. The planets include Mars Venus Earth Pluto and Mercury.
4. King Tut's tomb contained thrones statues jewelry vases and chariots.
5. The ancient Egyptians made mummies of dogs birds cats and crocodiles.
6. Mummies were bathed in perfume wrapped in cloth and sealed in hot wax.

Use a Comma After an Opening Phrase

Use a comma after an opening phrase or clause. Below are some examples. In each sentence, the introductory part is underlined.

> <u>Excited by the storm,</u> the dog barked madly.
> **phrase**

> <u>When it is so cold that you can see your breath,</u> you are actually seeing a little cloud.
> **dependent clause**

> <u>If the air is filled with moisture,</u> it will likely rain.
> **dependent clause**

Quick Quiz G

Directions: Add a comma after each opening phrase or clause.

1. Thrilled by the raise the custodian did an even better job.
2. Depressed over the pay cuts the workers started looking for other jobs.
3. Although Jim has to work overtime he can get to the soccer game.
4. Even though Pele hurt his knee he is still a good player.
5. If you enjoy soccer you should come to our games.

Answers to Quick Quizzes

Answers to Quick Quiz A

1. January 1, 2004
2. April 4, 1951
3. June 17, 2003
4. August 31, 2004
5. 3,000
6. 240,000
7. 51,000
8. 412,567

Answers to Quick Quiz B

1. We sent the package to 74 Adams Street, Arcadia, Florida 34266.
2. The party is being held at 190 Clark Road, Ammon, Idaho 83401.
3. There is an open house at 17 Main Street, Addison, Illinois 60101.
4. My sister just moved to 91-82 Fifth Boulevard, Muncie, Indiana 47302.
5. Wait until you see the house at 10196 Willowbrook Avenue, Mayfield, Kentucky 42066.
6. My father is staying at 353 Lexington Street, Lewison, Maine 04240.

Answers to Quick Quiz C

1. Dear Aunt Felice,
2. $1,000
3. $5,000
4. $4,000
5. Very truly yours,

Answers to Quick Quiz D

1. The Moon constantly circles Earth, and Earth constantly circles the Sun.
2. Earth spins very fast, but we do not ever feel it.
3. Amy studies the solar system, for she wants to be an astronaut.
4. She will take a lot of science in school, so she is well prepared.
5. This summer, she is going to space camp, or she will take some extra classes.
6. Amy knows this will be difficult, yet she is determined to succeed.

Answers to Quick Quiz E

1. "I will be late tonight because of the party," Ruth said.

2. Ruth said, "I will be late tonight because of the party."

3. "I will be late tonight," Ruth said, "because of the party."

4. "Don't forget that I have to take Ralph to the doctor," Robbie said.

5. Robbie said, "Don't forget that I have to take Ralph to the doctor."

6. "Don't forget," Robbie said, "that I have to take Ralph to the doctor."

Answers to Quick Quiz F

1. Earth's crust contains nickel, iron, and rock.

2. Venus is so hot that lead, tin, and zinc would melt there in a flash.

3. The planets include Mars, Venus, Earth, Pluto, and Mercury.

4. King Tut's tomb contained thrones, statues, jewelry, vases, and chariots.

5. The ancient Egyptians made mummies of dogs, birds, cats, and crocodiles.

6. Mummies were bathed in perfume, wrapped in cloth, and sealed in hot wax.

Answers to Quick Quiz G

1. Thrilled by the raise, the custodian did an even better job.

2. Depressed over the pay cuts, the workers started looking for other jobs.

3. Although Jim has to work overtime, he can get to the soccer game.

4. Even though Pele hurt his knee, he is still a good player.

5. If you enjoy soccer, you should come to our games.

Practice Test

Directions: Add commas as needed.

1. The planet Mercury travels at 107000 miles per hour.

2. The surprise birthday party will be held March 17 2004.

3. The couple's anniversary is June 28 2002.

4. The new stereo system cost $1249.

5. My aunt moved to 127 Powells Cove Boulevard Norton Massachusetts 02766.

6. We looked at an apartment at 346 Park Street Amory Mississippi 38821.

7. It is larger than the apartment at 891 A Intervale Avenue Camden New Hampshire 08101.

8. Marco Polo wrote about things that Europeans had never heard of such as paper money coal and asbestos.

9. The ancient Egyptians worshipped many gods, including these four: Osiris Isis Ra and Anubis.

10. There is nothing on television tonight so we will probably read a book.

11. It is fun to take a vacation but it often costs a lot of money.

12. "I wish there were more jobs in my field" Rikki said.

13. "I know how you feel" her sister said.

14. She answered "I have been out of work for almost a year now."

15. Thrilled by the unexpected gift the child jumped up and down.

16. Since the bus fare went up I walk to work more often.

17. If you like you could walk with me.

18. Because the street is quiet it is a very pleasant walk.

Answers

1. The planet Mercury travels at 107,000 miles per hour.

2. The surprise birthday party will be held March 17, 2004.

3. The couple's anniversary is June 28, 2002.

4. The new stereo system cost $1,249.

5. My aunt moved to 127 Powells Cove Boulevard, Norton, Massachusetts 02766.

6. We looked at an apartment at 346 Park Street, Amory, Mississippi 38821.

7. It is larger than the apartment at 891 A Intervale Avenue, Camden, New Hampshire 08101.

8. Marco Polo wrote about things that Europeans had never heard of, such as paper money, coal, and asbestos.

9. The ancient Egyptians worshipped many gods, including these four: Osiris, Isis, Ra, and Anubis.

10. There is nothing on television tonight, so we will probably read a book.

11. It is fun to take a vacation, but it often costs a lot of money.

12. "I wish there were more jobs in my field," Rikki said.

13. "I know how you feel," her sister said.

14. She answered, "I have been out of work for almost a year now."

15. Thrilled by the unexpected gift, the child jumped up and down.

16. Since the bus fare went up, I walk to work more often.

17. If you like, you could walk with me.

18. Because the street is quiet, it is a very pleasant walk.

Other Punctuation 16

In this chapter, you will learn how to use some of the other marks of punctuation in English.

The Period, Question Mark, and Exclamation Mark

Basically, the period, question mark, and exclamation mark are used at the end of a sentence. Do not combine any of these marks. For example, you cannot use an exclamation mark with a period. You cannot use a comma with a question mark. Consult this chart for examples:

Use One End Mark at a Time	
Incorrect	**Correct**
?.	?
!.	!
?!	?
!?	!
,?	?

Rule: Use a period after a complete sentence. Here are some examples:

- Last summer, I went to the beach.
- I had a good time.

Rule: Use a period after most abbreviations. If an abbreviation comes at the end of a sentence, do not add another period. Here are some examples:

- Dr.   Ms.   Jr.
- I admire Dr. Martin Luther King, Jr.

Rule: Use a question mark after a question. Here are some examples:

- Are you going out this weekend?
- Where are you going?

Rule: Use an exclamation mark after an exclamatory sentence. Here are some examples:

- What a beautiful car!
- Look at that amazing lion!

Quick Quiz A

Directions: Add periods, question marks, and exclamation marks as needed.

1. Where is the Ozark region
2. It is a big area in the south-central part of the United States
3. The Ozarks is such a beautiful area
4. In the spring, the family woke to a gentle rain
5. The birds chirped and the leaves swayed in the breeze
6. What is Gary's job
7. He works as a carpenter and a handyman
8. He works on construction jobs all over the world
9. Have you ever met such a hard worker
10. He is amazing

The Semicolon

A semicolon looks like this ;

There is a period on the top and a comma on the bottom. This combination tells you that a semicolon is stronger than a comma but not as strong as a period.

Rule: Use a semicolon between main clauses when the coordinating conjunction has been left out. Here are some examples:

- Jana is a good friend; she is always there for me.
- Antoine misplaced his wallet; he found it the next day.

Rule: Use a semicolon between main clauses connected by conjunctive adverbs such as *however, nevertheless, thus, moreover, for example,* and *consequently.* You learned about conjunctive adverbs in Chapter 6. Here are some examples:

- The campsite was crowded; nevertheless, we got a good spot.
- The shirt is expensive; however, it is very well made.

Quick Quiz B

Directions: Add semicolons as needed.

1. It's hard to imagine a world without libraries however, they haven't been around as long as you may think.
2. In the early 1700s, books were very expensive only the rich could afford to buy them.
3. There were no libraries consequently, few people had access to books.
4. Ben Franklin started a lending library thus, everyone could borrow books.
5. The first lending library opened in 1739 it was a great success.
6. Soon, other towns opened lending libraries as a result, everyone could get free access to books.
7. Reference librarians answer more than seven million questions every week that's a lot of questions!
8. Some people borrow books others take out movies.
9. Many people come to libraries for special programs children's story time is very popular.
10. Libraries are a precious resource consequently, we must never take them for granted.

The Colon

A colon looks like this :

It looks like one period stacked on top of another one. The colon and semicolon may look a little alike, but they are very different marks of punctuation.

Rule: Use a colon after the opening of a business letter. Here are some examples:

- Dear Ms. Robinson:
- Dear Dr. Hermann:
- To Whom It May Concern:
- Ladies and Gentlemen:

Rule: Use a colon before a list. Often, the word *following* will be used to introduce a list. Here are some examples:

- The new ice cream parlor offered the following flavors: blueberry, banana, and raspberry.

- We need the following supplies: glue, tape, and paper.

- The company makes the following products: belts, shoelaces, and batteries.

Use a colon before a long quotation, especially a formal one. Here is an example:

- John F. Kennedy said: "Ask not what your country can do for you—ask what you can do for your country."

Quick Quiz C

Directions: Add colons as needed.

1. Dear President Johnson
2. Dear Store Manager
3. To Whom It May Concern
4. I cleaned the following rooms the kitchen, the bathroom, and the basement.
5. Ms. Garcia can play the following instruments flute, piano, and organ.
6. James Russell Lowell said "The foolish and the dead alone never change their opinions."

Quotation Marks

Quotation marks are always used in pairs, like this " ". They have several different uses.

Rule: Use quotation marks to set off a speaker's exact words. Here are some examples:

- Ann said, "Can I borrow your pen?"
- "Can I borrow your pen?" Ann said.
- "If you can't find the store," Bill said, "call me on your cell phone."

If you are just talking about someone's words, do not use quotation marks. Someone else's words are called *indirect quotations*. Here are some examples:

Using Quotation Marks Correctly	
Indirect Quotations	**Direct Quotations**
Bob said that he will be late.	"I will be late," Bob said.
Terri said that she lost her job.	Terri said, "I lost my job."
Adam said the bus was late.	"The bus was late," Adam said.
Lara said that she likes Mexican food.	"I like Mexican food," Lara said.

Rule: Use quotation marks to set off the titles of short works such as poems, essays, songs, short stories, and magazine articles. (Underline long works such as novels, movies, and plays.) Here are some examples:

- Poems   "Annabel Lee"   "After Apple Picking"
- Essays   "Self-Reliance"   "The American Scholar"
- Songs   "Happy Birthday"   "America the Beautiful"
- Short stories   "The Black Cat"   "The Ransom of Red Chief"
- Magazine articles   "Fifty Beauty Secrets"   "Fixing Your Truck"

Quick Quiz D

Directions: Add quotation marks as necessary.

1. Will you be late? Martha asked.
2. I should be on time, Leslie answered.
3. Christa said that she will bring the books.
4. It is important that we study for the GED, Harris said.
5. Farah added, We want to be sure to do well.
6. The teacher said that we need to know grammar.
7. Tameka asked, Did you watch the new television show?
8. The Rime of the Ancient Mariner is a poem.
9. The Swimmer is a famous short story.
10. The Star-Spangled Banner is our national anthem.

Answers to Quick Quizzes

Answers to Quick Quiz A

1. Where is the Ozark region?
2. It is a big area in the south-central part of the United States.
3. The Ozarks is such a beautiful area!
4. In the spring, the family woke to a gentle rain.
5. The birds chirped and the leaves swayed in the breeze.
6. What is Gary's job?
7. He works as a carpenter and a handyman.
8. He works on construction jobs all over the world.
9. Have you ever met such a hard worker?
10. He is amazing!

Answers to Quick Quiz B

1. It's hard to imagine a world without libraries; however, they haven't been around as long as you may think.
2. In the early 1700s, books were very expensive; only the rich could afford to buy them.
3. There were no libraries; consequently, few people had access to books.
4. Ben Franklin started a lending library; thus, everyone could borrow books.
5. The first lending library opened in 1739; it was a great success.
6. Soon, other towns opened lending libraries; as a result, everyone could get free access to books.
7. Reference librarians answer more than seven million questions every week; that's a lot of questions!
8. Some people borrow books; others take out movies.
9. Many people come to libraries for special programs; children's story time is very popular.
10. Libraries are a precious resource; consequently, we must never take them for granted.

Answers to Quick Quiz C

1. Dear President Johnson:

2. Dear Store Manager:

3. To Whom It May Concern:

4. I cleaned the following rooms: the kitchen, the bathroom, and the basement.

5. Ms. Garcia can play the following instruments: flute, piano, and organ.

6. James Russell Lowell said: "The foolish and the dead alone never change their opinions."

Answers to Quick Quiz D

1. "Will you be late?" Martha asked.

2. "I should be on time," Leslie answered.

3. No quotation marks necessary.

4. "It is important that we study for the GED," Harris said.

5. Farah added, "We want to be sure to do well."

6. No quotation marks necessary.

7. Tameka asked, "Did you watch the new television show?"

8. "The Rime of the Ancient Mariner" is a poem.

9. "The Swimmer" is a famous short story.

10. "The Star-Spangled Banner" is our national anthem.

Practice Test

Directions: Add periods, question marks, and exclamation marks as needed.

1. Is there a doctor in the house
2. Tim got a new job
3. He will be working with his father
4. The job is in construction
5. What a great job
6. Do you think he will like the job
7. Tim will be working in the city
8. What a super idea
9. Are there any other jobs available
10. Construction is hard work but steady

Directions: Add semicolons and colons as needed.

11. Marci left for the party Bill decided to stay home.
12. We wanted to get a good grade therefore, we studied every day.
13. My brother joined the Marines last year he signed on for four years.
14. Jenette left the coffee pot on the stove consequently, it cracked.
15. Andy received the following gifts a toaster, an iron, an ironing board, and a blender.

Directions: Add quotation marks as needed.

16. I can't believe you ate the whole thing! she said.
17. He answered, I was hungry.
18. But you ate an entire pizza, she said.
19. You should not have left it on the counter, he answered.
20. Well, she replied, at least you cleaned up after yourself.

Answers

1. Is there a doctor in the house?

2. Tim got a new job.

3. He will be working with his father.

4. The job is in construction.

5. What a great job!

6. Do you think he will like the job?

7. Tim will be working in the city.

8. What a super idea!

9. Are there any other jobs available?

10. Construction is hard work but steady.

11. Marci left for the party; Bill decided to stay home.

12. We wanted to get a good grade; therefore, we studied every day.

13. My brother joined the Marines last year; he signed on for four years.

14. Jenette left the coffee pot on the stove; consequently, it cracked.

15. Andy received the following gifts: a toaster, an iron, an ironing board, and a blender.

16. "I can't believe you ate the whole thing!" she said.

17. He answered, "I was hungry."

18. "But you ate an entire pizza," she said.

19. "You should not have left it on the counter," he answered.

20. "Well," she replied, "at least you cleaned up after yourself."

Capitalization 17

Capitalization serves many important purposes. First, it tells readers when a new sentence is starting. Capitalization also points out specific words within a sentence. These words include *proper nouns*—nouns that name a specific person, place, or thing. In this chapter, you will learn the rules of capitalization.

Capitalize the First Word in a Sentence

Rule: Capitalize the first word in a sentence. This rule also covers dialogue, a speaker's exact words. Here are some examples:

- The plot is the structure of a story.
- Poems have rhythm and rhyme.
- "Are you taking the GED this year?" she asked.

Quick Quiz A

Directions: Circle the correct word to complete each sentence.

1. (according, According) to the latest census, Dade County is the largest county in Florida.
2. (The, the) Everglades became a national park in 1934.
3. "(Did, did) you ever visit Orlando, Florida?" the travel agent asked.
4. (My, my) brother-in-law lives in Florida.
5. (many, Many) people visit Florida every year.

Capitalize Proper Nouns and Proper Adjectives

Rule: Capitalize proper nouns and proper adjectives. Here are some examples:

- <u>Proper nouns</u>:   Italy   Haiti
- <u>Proper adjectives</u>:   Italian   Haitian

Rule: Capitalize a person's name. Here are some examples:

- Whitney Houston   Yao Ming
- Whoopi Goldberg   Roberto Clemente

Rule: Capitalize the title <u>before</u> a person's name. Here are some examples:

- Ms.   Mr.   Reverend
- Dr.   Professor   Miss

Rule: Capitalize abbreviations <u>after</u> a person's name. Here are some examples:

- Martin Luther King, Jr.   Beth Jobs, M.D.

Quick Quiz B

Directions: Choose the correct word in each line.

1.   Iranian   iranian
2.   halle berry   Halle Berry
3.   dr. pepper   Dr. Pepper
4.   Queen Latifah   queen latifah
5.   Shoshana Goldish, M.D.   Shoshana Goldish, m.d.
6.   ms. Nolan   Ms. Nolan

Rule: Capitalize the names of organizations, institutions, courses, and famous buildings. That's because these are all proper nouns. Here are some examples:

- <u>Organizations</u>: Boy Scouts USA   The Girl Scouts of America
- <u>Institutions</u>: The United Nations   Major League Baseball
- <u>Courses</u>:   French 101   Mathematics 203
                        (but not mathematics)
- <u>Buildings</u>:   Taj Mahal   Sphinx

Quick Quiz C

Directions: Add capital letters as needed. The number in parentheses ( ) indicates the number of capital letters needed.

1. the statue of liberty is the largest freestanding sculpture ever created. (3)

2. It was given by the people of france to the people of the united states as a symbol of a shared love of freedom and everlasting friendship. (3)

3. it weighs 450,000 pounds and rises 151 feet above its pedestal. (1)

4. more than 100 feet around, ms. liberty boasts eyes two and a half feet wide, a mouth three feet wide, and a nose four and a half feet long. (3)

5. her upraised right arm extends forty-two feet; her hand is nearly seventeen feet long. (1)

Rule: Capitalize days, months, and holidays. That's because these are all proper nouns. Here are some examples:

- <u>Days:</u>   Monday   Tuesday   Wednesday
- <u>Months:</u>   February   March   April
- <u>Holidays:</u> Thanksgiving Fourth of July Valentine's Day

Quick Quiz D

Directions: Choose the correct word in each line.

1. Thursday   thursday
2. mother's day   Mother's Day
3. Saturday   saturday
4. september   September
5. June   june
6. presidents' day   Presidents' Day

Rule: Capitalize geographical places and sections of the country. That's because these are all proper nouns. Here are some examples:

- <u>Geographical places:</u>   Europe   Asia   Argentina
- <u>Sections of the country:</u> the South   the Midwest   the North

Rule: Capitalize the names of specific historical events, eras, and documents. That's because these are all proper nouns. Do not capitalize small words like *a, an,* and *the,* unless they are part of the title. Here are some examples:

- <u>Historical events:</u>   Declaration of Independence   Great Depression
- <u>Historical eras:</u>   Dark Ages   Renaissance
- <u>Historical documents:</u> Constitution   Bill of Rights

Quick Quiz E

Directions: Capitalize each of the following words and phrases correctly. Write your answers on the line.

1. revolutionary war _____
2. magna carta _____
3. korean war _____
4. civil war _____
5. jazz age _____
6. harlem renaissance _____

Rule: Capitalize the names of languages, nationalities, countries, and races. That's because these are all proper nouns. Here are some examples:

- <u>Languages:</u>   English   French   Creole
- <u>Nationalities:</u>   American   Israeli   South African
- <u>Countries:</u>   Ghana   Chile   China
- <u>Races:</u>   Asian   Native-American   African-American

Rule: Capitalize religions and references to the Supreme Being, including the pronouns referring to the Supreme Being. That's because these are all proper nouns. Here are some examples:

- <u>Religions:</u>   Judaism   Catholicism   Islam
- <u>Religious references:</u> the Creator   Him   Heaven

Quick Quiz F

Directions: Capitalize each of the following words and phrases correctly. Write your answers on the line.

1. spanish _____
2. german _____
3. czech republic _____
4. african _____
5. christian scientist _____
6. god _____

Capitalize Parts of Letters

Rule: Capitalize the greeting in a letter. Here are some examples:

- Dear Ms. O'Connor: Dear Aunt Ethel,
- Dear Mr. Urick:Dear Fred,

Rule: Capitalize the first letter of the first word in the closing of a letter. Do not capitalize the other words. Here are some examples:

- Sincerely yours,
- Yours very truly,

Quick Quiz G

Directions: Choose the correct word in each line.

1. Dear Dr. Carvo: dear dr. Carvo:
2. dear Hester,   Dear Hester,
3. Yours Truly,   Yours truly,
4. Best wishes,   Best Wishes,

Capitalize Titles

Rule: Capitalize the titles of books, plays, newspapers, and magazines. Do not capitalize the small words like *a, an,* and *the,* unless they begin the title. Here are some examples:

- Book titles: *Like Water for Chocolate*   *For Whom the Bell Tolls*
- Play titles: *The Agony and the Ecstasy*   *Hairspray*
- Newspaper titles: *The Cleveland Plain Dealer*   *The Los Angeles Times*
- Magazine titles: *Seventeen*   *Road and Track*

Quick Quiz H

Directions: Capitalize each of the following titles correctly. Write your answers on the line.

1. *the great gatsby* _____
2. *the lion, the witch, and the wardrobe* _____
3. *heartbreak house* _____
4. *our town* _____
5. *the chicago tribune* _____
6. *people* magazine _____

Answers to Quick Quizzes

Answers to Quick Quiz A

1. According
2. The
3. Did
4. My
5. Many

Answers to Quick Quiz B

1. Iranian
2. Halle Berry
3. Dr. Pepper
4. Queen Latifah
5. Shoshana Goldish, M.D.
6. Ms. Nolan

Answers to Quick Quiz C

1. The Statue of Liberty is the largest freestanding sculpture ever created.
2. It was given by the people of France to the people of the United States as a symbol of a shared love of freedom and everlasting friendship.
3. It weighs 450,000 pounds and rises 151 feet above its pedestal.
4. More than 100 feet around, Ms. Liberty boasts eyes two and a half feet wide, a mouth three feet wide, and a nose four and a half feet long.
5. Her upraised right arm extends forty-two feet; her hand is nearly seventeen feet long.

Answers to Quick Quiz D

1. Thursday
2. Mother's Day
3. Saturday
4. September
5. June
6. Presidents' Day

Answers to Quick Quiz E

1. Revolutionary War
2. Magna Carta
3. Korean War
4. Civil War
5. Jazz Age
6. Harlem Renaissance

Answers to Quick Quiz F

1. Spanish
2. German
3. Czech Republic
4. African
5. Christian Scientist
6. God

Answers to Quick Quiz G

1. Dear Dr. Carvo:
2. Dear Hester,
3. Yours truly,
4. Best wishes,

Answers to Quick Quiz H

1. *The Great Gatsby*
2. *The Lion, the Witch, and the Wardrobe*
3. *Heartbreak House*
4. *Our Town*
5. *The Chicago Tribune*
6. *People* magazine

Practice Test

Directions: Add capital letters as needed. The number in parentheses ( ) indicates the number of capital letters that you need.

1. this season, the new york mets are on a winning streak. (4)

2. the mets play at shea stadium in flushing, new york. (7)

3. During the June 3 game against the cubs, catcher mike piazza made another superb throw. (3)

4. player mo vaughn got a good jump on the cubs' pitcher. (4)

5. "we're proud of the mets," said a major league baseball representative. (5)

6. mayor mike bloomberg and reverend al sharpton enjoyed the game. (6)

7. They ate italian ices and french fries. (2)

8. egypt is a long fertile strip of land in northeastern africa. (2)

9. back then, all the water came from the nile river. (3)

10. around 300 BC, high egyptian officials authorized the building of the first pyramids. (2)

11. egypt is located in africa. (2)

12. deserts to the east and west cut off egypt from the rest of the world. (2)

13. there were dangerous rapids on the nile to the south. (2)

14. this isolation allowed the egyptians to work in peace and security. (2)

15. ancient egypt had an abundance of limestone, sandstone, and granite. (2)

16. workers brought these rocks from quarries to the building sites. (1)

17. egypt's most precious resource—the great nile river–provided the means for transportation. (3)

Answers

1. This season, the New York Mets are on a winning streak.

2. The Mets play at Shea Stadium in Flushing, New York.

3. During the June 3 game against the Cubs, catcher Mike Piazza made another superb throw.

4. Mo Vaughn got a good jump on the Cubs' pitcher.

5. "We're proud of the Mets," said a Major League Baseball representative.

6. Mayor Mike Bloomberg and Reverend Al Sharpton enjoyed the game.

7. They ate Italian ices and French fries.

8. Egypt is a long fertile strip of land in northeastern Africa.

9. Back then, all the water came from the Nile River.

10. Around 300 B.C., high Egyptian officials authorized the building of the first pyramids.

11. Egypt is located in Africa.

12. Deserts to the east and west cut off Egypt from the rest of the world.

13. There were dangerous rapids on the Nile to the south.

14. This isolation allowed the Egyptians to work in peace and security.

15. Ancient Egypt had an abundance of limestone, sandstone, and granite.

16. Workers brought these rocks from quarries to the building sites.

17. Egypt's most precious resource—the great Nile River—provided the means for transportation.

Reevaluating Your Skills

Posttest

Parts of Speech

Directions: Sort the following words according to their parts of speech. Write the words on the chart below.

although	anxiety	because	follow	
your	and	yet	edge	recognize
droop	me	pizza	either...or	
anyone	Marla	them	team	you
but	dig	are being	their	
sixty-six	feel			

Nouns	Verbs	Pronouns	Conjunctions
_____	_____	_____	_____
_____	_____	_____	_____
_____	_____	_____	_____
_____	_____	_____	_____
_____	_____	_____	_____
_____	_____	_____	_____

Directions: Identify the part of speech of each underlined word. Write your answers on the lines.

Between (1) <u>Homedale</u> and Lewiston, Idaho, the Snake River (2) <u>twists</u> its way north, separating Oregon (3) <u>and</u> Idaho. This (4) <u>river</u> (5) <u>flows</u> through Hells Canyon. To the east, the Seven Devils Range in Idaho towers 8,000 feet above the river. (6) <u>They</u> are beautiful! From the crest of the ridges, (7) <u>you</u> can see pretty, grassy plateau country (8) <u>and</u> tumbling masses of mountains. (9) <u>Tourists</u> come from miles around to enjoy the gorgeous view. Hells Canyon is one of (10) <u>America's</u> most beautiful places.

1. _____

2. _____

3. _____

4. _____

5. _____

6. _____

7. _____

8. _____

9. _____

10. _____

More Parts of Speech

Directions: Sort the words according to their parts of speech. Write the words on the chart below.

my dear	nevertheless	green	quickly	slowly
above	wow	near-sighted	first	ouch
oh	yesterday	below	inside	gee
enough	now	within	any	into
the	below	underneath	gosh	

Adjectives	Adverbs	Prepositions	Interjections
_____	_____	_____	_____
_____	_____	_____	_____
_____	_____	_____	_____
_____	_____	_____	_____
_____	_____	_____	_____
_____	_____	_____	_____

Directions: Identify the part of speech of each underlined word. Write your answers on the lines provided.

In the summer of 1993, (1) <u>incredible</u> amounts of rain fell on the Midwest. At times, an inch of rain fell (2) <u>every</u> six minutes. The flood appears to have been caused in part (3) <u>by</u> El Niño. This brought (4) <u>heavy</u> (5) <u>winter</u> rains. The (6) <u>cool</u> summer of 1992 resulted (7) <u>in</u> less evaporation. (8) <u>Wow!</u> The land could hardly absorb more water. Floodwaters rose up and down the basin (9) <u>of</u> the Mississippi River. More than eight billion dollars worth of property was (10) <u>badly</u> damaged.

1. _____

2. _____

3. _____

4. _____

5. _____

6. _____

7. _____

8. _____

9. _____

10. _____

Sentences

Directions: Write **P** for each word group that is a phrase.

_____ **1.** a beautiful red rose

_____ **2.** The sheep are in the pen.

_____ **3.** near the bus stop

_____ **4.** Small planets have weak gravity.

_____ **5.** over the bridge by the lake

_____ **6.** I am taking my GED.

_____ **7.** eating slowly and carefully

_____ **8.** Twelve people have set foot on the moon.

Directions: Write **C** for each word group that is a clause.

_____ **9.** In the car

_____ **10.** Even if you do not agree with my opinion

_____ **11.** Next to the diner

_____ **12.** The Sun is at the center of the solar system.

_____ **13.** Luck

_____ **14.** There is no life on the moon.

_____ **15.** Clouds help trap heat.

_____ **16.** Because the GED can help you get a good job

Directions: Label each sentence as a simple sentence, a compound sentence, or a complex sentence.

_____ **17.** Lightning strikes in the U.S. about 40 million times a year.

_____ **18.** The dog is afraid of lightning, but the cat is not frightened.

_____ **19.** Because it snowed a lot, roads were closed.

_____ **20.** Never stand under a tree during a storm.

_____ **21.** If you see a tornado coming, you should take shelter.

_____ **22.** The hurricane caused much damage, but no one was hurt.

_____ **23.** When a blizzard is predicted, be sure to bring your snow shovels inside.

_____ **24.** Tornadoes are the worst storms of all.

_____ **25.** The storm was fierce, and the power lines blew down.

_____ **26.** Storms cause a lot of damage.

Common Grammar Problems

Directions: Correct all sentence errors. You will find run-ons and fragments. Write the corrected sentence on the lines provided.

1. Parents yelled at their kids during the game the coaches got angry.

   _____

   _____

2. The coaches started to scream the parents would not back off.

   _____

   _____

3. Because the parents could not control themselves.

   _____

   _____

4. Assigned blame to the other.

   _____

   _____

5. Was very unpleasant.

   _____

   _____

Directions: Choose the correct word to complete each sentence.

6. In his free time, Jose (give, gives) blood.

7. The workers (store, stores) their gear in a locker.

8. Dr. Calabro (smiles, smile) when she (see, sees) me.

9. I (does, do) all my reading at night.

10. You (have, has) some cat fur on your shirt.

Directions: Correct all errors with dangling and misplaced modifiers. Write the corrected sentences on the lines provided.

11. Reaching the top of the hill, the view was beautiful.

_____

_____

12. To get into the movies, an ID must be presented.

_____

_____

13. To find a good deal, time must be spent comparing prices.

_____

_____

14. The teacher explained why misplaced modifiers are wrong on Monday.

_____

_____

15. The ceiling was dripping water by the time I called a plumber in the basement.

_____

_____

Directions: Correct all double negatives errors. Write the corrected sentences on the lines provided.

16. He never had no time to rest.

_____

_____

17. My boss does not give me nothing.

_____

_____

18. There aren't hardly any chips left.

_____

_____

19. Jesse didn't never study.

_____

_____

20. Nobody showed up for none of the practices.

_____

_____

Mechanics

Directions: Add commas where they belong.

1. We used to live at 333 Northern Avenue Lake Oswego Oregon 97034.
2. My uncle lives at 7 Cove Street Saddle River New Jersey 07458.
3. July 4 1776 is the birthday of America's freedom.
4. We are going to Las Vegas on May 1 2004.
5. The trip will cost between $2500 and $3000.
6. We plan to see the hotels first and then we will visit Hoover Dam.
7. The trip should be fun but we have a lot of work to do as well.
8. We are getting trained for a new program so we have to stay alert.
9. "I hope you have fun" my friend Jamal said.
10. "I will have a great time" I answered.

Directions: Correct all errors in punctuation. Add periods, question marks, exclamation marks, semicolons, colons, and quotation marks as they are needed.

11. My family is having a picnic
12. Over 200 people are coming
13. Can you join us
14. About half the guests are coming from Georgia the rest are from North Carolina.
15. My mother's aunts are singers consequently, we will have some great music.
16. My father's brothers are good athletes as a result, we will have a baseball game.
17. Buy the following items for the picnic potato salad, cole slaw, and macaroni salad.
18. Benjamin Disraeli said "Change is inevitable in a progressive country. Change is constant."
19. Please take out the trash, Bernie said.
20. Song of Myself is a famous poem.

Directions: Correct all errors in capitalization. The number in parentheses ( ) tells you the number of capitalization errors.

21. in 1950, 400 american sportswriters selected jim thorpe as the greatest athlete of the first half of the 20th century. (4)
22. a sac and fox indian, thorpe was born in oklahoma in 1888. (6)
23. he stunned the entire world with his brilliant performance at the 1912 olympic games in stockholm. (4)
24. A year later, the olympic committee learned that thorpe had accepted money to play baseball in north carolina. (5)
25. many people feel that thorpe had been treated unfairly. (2)

Answers

Answers to Parts of Speech

Nouns	Verbs	Pronoun	Conjunctions
edge	droop	me	either...or
team	recognize	you	and
pizza	follow	anyone	but
Marla	dig	them	although
anxiety	are being	their	because
sixty-six	feel	your	yet

1. noun
2. verb
3. conjunction
4. noun
5. verb
6. pronoun
7. pronoun
8. conjunction
9. noun
10. noun

Answers to More Parts of Speech

Adjectives	Adverbs	Prepositions	Interjections
green	quickly	above	wow
first	slowly	below	ouch
enough	now	inside	gee
below	underneath	gosh	oh
any	yesterday	within	my dear
near-sighted	nevertheless	into	

1. adjective
2. adverb
3. preposition
4. adverb
5. adjective
6. adjective
7. preposition
8. interjection
9. preposition
10. adverb

Answers to Sentences

The correct answers are 1, 3, 5, and 7.
The correct answers are 11, 12, 14, 15, and 16.

17. simple sentence
18. compound sentence
19. complex sentence
20. simple sentence
21. complex sentence
22. compound sentence
23. complex sentence
24. simple sentence
25. compound sentence
26. simple sentence.

Answers to Common Grammar Problems

1. Parents yelled at their kids during the game, so the coaches got angry.

2. The coaches started to scream, but the parents would not back off.

3. Because the parents could not control themselves, they were asked to leave.

4. Each side assigned blame to the other.

5. The day was very unpleasant.

6. gives

7. store

8. smiles, sees

9. do

10. have

11. When we reached the top of the hill, the view was beautiful.

12. To get into the movies, you must present an ID.

13. To find a good deal, you must spend time comparing prices.

14. On Monday, the teacher explained why misplaced modifiers are wrong.

15. The ceiling was dripping water in the basement by the time I called a plumber.

16. He never had time to rest.

17. My boss does not give me anything.

18. There are hardly any chips left.

19. Jesse didn't ever study.

20. Nobody showed up for any of the practices.

Answers to Mechanics

1. We used to live at 333 Northern Avenue, Lake Oswego, Oregon 97034.
2. My uncle lives at 7 Cove Street, Saddle River, New Jersey 07458.
3. July 4, 1776, is the birthday of America's freedom.
4. We are going to Las Vegas on May 1, 2004.
5. The trip will cost between $2,500 and $3,000.
6. We plan to see the hotels first, and then we will visit Hoover Dam.
7. The trip should be fun, but we have a lot of work to do as well.
8. We are getting trained for a new program, so we have to stay alert.
9. "I hope you have fun," my friend Jamal said.
10. "I will have a great time," I answered.
11. My family is having a picnic.
12. Over 200 people are coming!
13. Can you join us?
14. About half the guests are coming from Georgia; the rest are from North Carolina.
15. My mother's aunts are singers; consequently, we will have some great music.
16. My father's brothers are good athletes; as a result, we will have a baseball game.
17. Buy the following items for the picnic: potato salad, cole slaw, and macaroni salad.
18. Benjamin Disraeli said: "Change is inevitable in a progressive country. Change is constant."
19. "Please take out the trash," Bernie said.
20. "Song of Myself" is a famous poem.
21. In 1950, 400 American sportswriters selected Jim Thorpe as the greatest athlete of the first half of the 20th century.
22. A Sac and Fox Indian, Thorpe was born in Oklahoma in 1888.
23. He stunned the entire world with his brilliant performance at the 1912 Olympic Games in Stockholm.
24. A year later, the Olympic Committee learned that Thorpe had accepted money to play baseball in North Carolina.
25. Many people feel that Thorpe had been treated unfairly.

Appendices

About the GED

What to Expect on the GED

There are five GED tests:

- Language Arts, Writing
- Social Studies
- Science
- Language Arts, Reading
- Mathematics

On every test (except for Language Arts, Writing) all the questions will be multiple choice. Each multiple-choice question will have five possible answer choices. For each question, you must choose the best answer of the five possible choices. The multiple-choice questions may be based on a graphic, a text, or a mathematics problem, or they may just test your knowledge of a particular subject. Let's take a look at the kinds of questions asked on each subject area test.

Language Arts, Writing

The multiple-choice section of the Language Arts, Writing exam tests English grammar and usage. It contains several passages and questions about those passages in which you find errors or determine the best way to rewrite particular sentences. The essay section will require you to write a 200- to 250-word essay on a particular topic in 45 minutes. This question won't test your knowledge of a particular subject, such as the War of 1812 or the Pythagorean theorem. Instead, you will write about your own life experiences. The readers of the essay will not be grading the essay based on how much you know or don't know about the topic, but rather on how well you use standard English.

Social Studies

The Social Studies Test contains multiple-choice questions on history, economics, political science, and geography. In the United States, the test focuses on U.S. history and government, while the test in Canada focuses on Canadian history and government. World history will be included, too. Some of the questions will be based on reading passages, and some questions will be based on graphics such as maps, charts, illustrations, or political cartoons.

Science

The Science Test contains multiple-choice questions on physical and life sciences. You will also see questions on earth science, space science, life science, health science, and environmental science. As with the Social Studies Test, some of the Science Test questions will be based upon reading passages and some of the questions will be based upon graphics such as scientific diagrams.

Language Arts, Reading

The Language Arts, Reading Test is similar to the Social Studies and Science Tests in that the multiple-choice questions will be based on passages. The questions will be based on longer passages than questions in the other subject area tests. In the Language Arts, Reading Test, some of the questions will be based on a poem, some on prose, some on a piece of drama, and some on documents that you might encounter in the workplace.

Mathematics

There are two parts to the Mathematics Test. You can use a calculator on Part I, but not on Part II. The Mathematics Test uses multiple-choice questions to measure your skills in arithmetic, algebra, geometry, and problem solving. Some of the questions will ask you to find the answer to a problem, while others will require you to find the best way to solve the problem. Many of the questions will be based upon diagrams. Some of the questions will be grouped into sets that require you to draw upon information from a number of sources, such as graphs and charts.

The majority of GED questions on all five of the tests measure your skills and test-taking abilities. What does this mean for you? This means that if you work hard to sharpen your test-taking skills, you will be much more prepared for success on the tests than if you sat down and memorized names, dates, facts, properties, charts, or other bits of information. Basically, you will have more success on the GED if you know how to take the tests—

instead of knowing all the information about reading, writing, science, social studies, and math. Let's look at some strategies for answering multiple-choice questions.

Answering Multiple-Choice Questions

The key to success on multiple-choice tests is understanding the questions and how to find the correct answer. Each multiple-choice question on the GED will be followed by five answer choices: 1, 2, 3, 4, and 5. There will be no trick questions and no questions intended to confuse you. If you use the strategies that follow, you will be successful on the multiple-choice questions.

Strategies for Answering Multiple-Choice Questions

- **Read the question carefully and make sure you know what it is asking.** Read each question slowly. If you rush through the question, you might miss a key word that could cost you the correct answer. You might want to run your pencil under the question as you read it to be sure that you don't miss anything in the question. If you don't understand the question after the first time you read it, go back and read it another time or two until you do understand it.

- **Don't overanalyze the question or read something into the question that just isn't there.** Many test-takers make the mistake of overanalyzing questions, looking for some trick or hidden meaning that the test-creators added for the sake of confusion. The test-creators didn't do that on any of the questions on the GED, so take each question at face value. Each question will say exactly what it means, so don't try to interpret something that isn't there.

- **Circle or underline the key words in the question.** As you read through the question, locate any important words in the question and either circle or underline the word or words. Important words will be anything taken directly from the chart, table, graph, or reading passage on which the question is based. Other important words will be words like *compare, contrast, similar, different,* or *main idea.* By circling or underlining the key words, you will understand the question better and will be more prepared to recognize the correct answer.

- **After you read the question, try to answer the question in your head before you look at the answer choices.** If you think you know the answer to the question without even looking at the answer choices, then you most likely will recognize the correct answer right away when you read the possible answer choices. Also, if you think you know the correct answer right away, then you should be very confident in your answer when you find it listed among the possible answer choices.

- **Try covering the answer choices while you are reading the question.** To try answering the question in your head without being influenced by the answer choices, cover the answer choices with your hand as you read the question. This technique will also help prevent you from reading something into the question that isn't there based on something you saw in one of the answer choices first. Covering the answer choices may also help you concentrate only on the question to make sure you read it carefully and correctly.

- **Carefully read all the answer choices before answering the question.** You need to look at all the possibilities before you choose the best or correct answer. Even if you think you know the answer before looking at the possible answer choices, read all of the answer choices anyway. If you read through two of the answer choices and you find that choice (3) is a good answer, keep reading because (4) or (5) may very well be a better answer. Finally, by reading all the answer choices, you can be more confident in your answer because you will see that the other choices are definitely incorrect.

- **Eliminate answer choices that you know are wrong.** As you read through all the choices, some will obviously be incorrect. When you find those answer choices, cross them out. This will help you narrow the possible choices. In addition, crossing out incorrect answers will prevent you from choosing an incorrect answer by mistake.

- **Don't spend too much time on one question.** If you read a question and you just can't seem to find the best or correct answer, circle the question, skip it, and come back to it later. Your time will be better spent on questions that you can answer. Your time is limited, so don't struggle with one question if you could correctly answer three others in the same amount of time.

- **Go with your first answer.** Once you choose an answer, stick to it. A test-taker's first hunch is usually the correct one. There is a reason why your brain told you to choose a particular answer, so stand by it. Also, don't waste time debating over whether the answer you chose is correct. Go with your first answer and move on.

- **Don't go back and change your answer unless you have a good, solid reason to do so.** Remember that your first hunch is usually the best, so don't change your answer on a whim. One of the only times you should change your answer on a previous question is if you find something later in the test that contradicts what you chose. The only other time you should change an answer is if you remember very clearly a teacher's lecture, a reading passage, or some other reliable source of information to the contrary of what you chose.

- **Look for hints within the answer choices.** For example, some sets of answer choices may contain two choices that vary by only a word or two. Chances are that the correct answer is one of those two answers.

- **Watch out for absolutes.** Other hints within answer choices can be words called absolutes. These words include *always*, *never*, *only*, or *completely*. These words severely limit the possibility of that answer choice being right.

- **If you just don't know the correct answer, guess.** That's right, guess. The GED Tests are scored based on how many questions you answer correctly, and there is no point penalty for answering incorrectly. Therefore, why leave questions unanswered? If you do, you have no chance at getting any points for those. However, if you guess, you at least have a chance to get some points. Before you guess, try to eliminate as many wrong answer choices as possible. You have a much greater chance of choosing the correct answer if you can weed out some that are incorrect. This strategy is especially helpful if you have several questions left for which you are going to guess.

- **Be aware of how much time you have left on the test.** However, don't glance down at your watch or up at the clock after every question to check the time. You will be instructed at the beginning of the test as to the amount of time you have to complete the test. Just be aware of that amount of time. The creators of the GED Tests designed the tests and the test times so that you will have ample time to complete the tests. As you approach the point at which you have 10 minutes left, make sure that you are not spending your time answering the difficult questions if you still have other questions ahead of you that you can easily answer. If you have answered all the questions that you can with relatively little difficulty, go back and work on those that gave you trouble. If you come down to the wire and have a few left, guess at the answers.

- **If you have time left at the end of the test, go back to any questions that you skipped.** After you finish all the questions that you can answer without too much difficulty, you should go back over the test and find the ones you skipped. The amount of time you have left should determine the amount of time you spend on each unanswered question. For example, if you have 10 questions left and 10 minutes left, try to work on a few of them. However, if you have 10 questions left and 2 minutes left, go through and guess on each of the remaining questions.

What's Next?

Working with this book is the first step toward getting your GED. But what should you do next? Many people find it helpful to take a GED test-preparation course. Call your local high school counselor or the Adult Education or Continuing Education Department at your local community college, college, or university. The people in those offices can tell you where courses are offered and how to enroll. In addition to taking a GED course, continue studying on your own with this book and others in the ARCO line of books.

Once you feel ready to take the tests, contact the GED Testing Service to find out when and where the exams will be administered next:

General Educational Development
GED Testing Service
American Council on Education
One Dupont Circle, NW, Suite 250
Washington, D.C. 20036
800-626-9433 (toll-free)

www.gedtest.org

Good luck!

Idiom List and Word Formation B

Here's a list of some of the idioms that English-speaking high school students should know (though it isn't a complete list of every idiom. Whenever you see an idiom for the first time, add it to this list and memorize it so you can use it and recognize it in the future.

Idioms are often the most difficult things to learn when you are learning a language because sometimes they don't make much sense. If you think about it, why do we say "according to" and not "according from"? If English is not your first language, you should be extra diligent about studying this list. Even if it is your first language, pay close attention so that you don't misuse an idiom.

able to, ability to

Grandpa is no longer able to juggle chainsaws the way he used to.
Turtles have the ability to sleep in their shells for weeks at a time.

access to

During the scandal, reporters were not given access to secret files.

according to

According to government sources, cheddar cheese is a very nutritious snack.

account for

France accounts for 70 percent of all red wine made throughout the world.

accuse of

During the war, Private Benjamin was accused of treason.

agree with

I don't agree with your opinion.

appear to

People who live in big cities often don't appear to be very friendly.

apply to

I'm going to apply to fifteen colleges this spring.

argue over

The roommates always argued over whose turn it was to wash the dishes.

as [adjective] as

My uncle is as smart as most nuclear physicists.

assure that

I assure you that I have never eaten a blueberry Pop Tart.

at a disadvantage

For many teenagers, living in poverty puts them at a disadvantage in school.

attempt to

The pole vaulter attempted to clear 15 feet.

attend to, attention to

Baby-sitters don't always attend to children as well as they should. The accountant was known for his attention to detail.

attribute to

Many clever quotes are attributed to Mark Twain.

available to

Is your aunt available to baby-sit on Friday night?

based on

The play was based on a true story.

because of

Because of the time difference, she had to call Paris at 3 a.m.

believed to be

He is believed to be the only living descendant of George Washington.

between [1] and [2]

Just between you and me, I think that movie was really bad.

call for

Old King Cole called for three fiddlers.

choice of

The airplane passengers were given a choice of chicken or fish for dinner.

choose to [verb]

Many people choose to attend vocational school rather than a four-year college.

choose from [nouns]

Students were offered the chance to choose from dozens of different science classes.

claim to

My cousin's claim to fame is that he once delivered a pizza to Robert De Niro.

considered or considered to be

Picasso is considered one of the world's finest abstract painters.
Picasso is considered to be one of the world's finest abstract painters.

consist of

The project consists of a paper, an oral presentation, and a scale model.

consistent with

The results of my experiment were consistent with those of my lab partner.

continue to

I called the police because my neighbor continued to play his stereo at top volume at 3 in the morning.

contrast with

Her wild dress and hip boots really contrasted with her date's polo shirt and khakis.

contribute to

We asked our Home Ec teacher to contribute some brownies to our tenth grade bake sale.

cost of [something]

The cost of a Big Mac is used to compare the rate of inflation.

cost to [someone]

If you order now, we'll throw in a bottle of our special Lime Juice Miracle, at no cost to you!

credit with

I'd like to credit my mother with teaching me how to whistle.

deal with

When I got home from school, the last thing I wanted to deal with was bubble gum on my shoes.

debate over

The debate over whether or not our school should start an hour earlier caused a riot at the school board meeting.

decide to (not decide on)

"We've decided to turn your room into a home gym as soon as you leave for college," my parents announced gleefully.

defend against

Atlanta tried to defend itself against Sherman's attack without success.

define as

Nationalism is defined as loyalty and devotion to a nation, according to *Meriam-Webster's Collegiate Dictionary.*

delighted by

I was delighted by the grade I received on my final exam in chemistry class.

demonstrate that

I used some coffee and some grape juice to demonstrate that Lime Juice Miracle can remove any stain from carpet.

depend on

Which college I attend depends on which colleges accept me.

descend from

The trapeze artist descended from the ceiling on a swing.

different from

My aspirations for the future are different from yours—I want to be a trapeze artist and you want to be an American idol.

difficult to

It is difficult to concentrate on my geometry homework when I can smell peach cobbler baking in the kitchen.

distinguish [1] from [2]

"I think I might be colorblind," said my brother. "I can't distinguish green from red."

draw on

She drew on all her years of experience as a teacher to get us to learn the words to "How Deep Is Your Love" in Spanish.

due to

Due to a scheduling error, our homecoming game was an away game.

[in an] effort to

In an effort to preserve water, the town council mandated a rule that residents could only water their lawns in the rain.

either...or

"Either I go or he goes!" my father shouted, pointing at my hamster.

encourage to

I encourage you to stay in school instead of dropping out.

–er than (taller than, bigger than, smarter than, etc.)

I am taller than anyone else in my gym class.

estimate to be

She is estimated to be older than 90, although no one knows for sure.

expose to

I was exposed to chicken pox three times before I finally caught it.

extent of

We only found out the extent of her obsession with marbles after she died and we could look in her closets.

fear that

She feared that if she wore the same shoes two days in a row no one would be her friend.

forbid to

"I forbid you to leave this house in that outfit!" screamed my mother.

force to

I had to force myself to eat the horrible-tasting cake at my birthday party.

frequency of

We discovered that the frequency of air conditioner thefts increased during the heat wave last year.

from [1] to [2]

I changed my ticket from today to Wednesday so I could go to the amusement park with my class.

in contrast to

In contrast to her previous boyfriend, her current boyfriend wore shoes when he was in public.

in danger of

He was in danger of causing a traffic accident when he walked around with no shirt on.

in order to

In order to graduate from high school, you have to pass your exit-level exam.

inclined to

I am not inclined to believe him after all the lies he told me about his family.

infected with

Once I was infected with chicken pox, I didn't know why I wanted to get it in the first place.

instead of

Instead of riding the bus to school, she decided to walk.

introduce to

My grandfather introduced me to his best friend from grade school.

isolate from

Students with learning disabilities sometimes feel isolated from everyone else in their classes.

just as . . . so too

Just as my parents grew up and got boring, so too will my sister some day.

less than

Even though she finished less than one half of the book, she still wrote a B+ book report.

likely to (also unlikely to)

I did not think she was likely to go to the prom with me after I tripped and spilled spaghetti sauce on her white blouse.

mistake for

You would never mistake me for a graceful ballet dancer.

more than

My cousin ate more pies than anyone else at the county fair.

move away from

My sister couldn't wait to move away from home, but now she comes over every night for dinner.

native to or a native of

This plant is native to Wyoming.
My teacher is a native of Wyoming, but she had never seen the plant before.

neither . . . nor

She ordered neither maple syrup nor chocolate sauce with her Belgian waffles.

not [1] but [2]

Not love but jealousy drove him to marry someone he'd only known for eight days.

not only . . . but also

He is not only a wonderful singer but also a black belt in karate.

on account of

We hid in the basement for 3 hours on account of the tornado warning.

opportunity for [noun]

"This seems like a perfect opportunity for mischief," said the teacher when she noticed that the gate was unlocked.

opportunity to [verb]

Whenever you have the opportunity to eat key lime pie, you should, in my opinion.

opposed to

I am opposed to any form of violence as discipline for children.

opposite of

The opposite of black is white.

permit to

The woman was not permitted to enter the deli with her poodle.

persuade to

It took all the ice cream in my freezer to persuade my friend to tell me the secret.

pressure to

Bruce Springsteen felt pressure to play all his old songs on his concert tour even though he was more interested in his new ones.

prevent from

Air bags are meant to prevent you from being injured in an auto accident.

prized by

Prized by collectors, the rare first edition of the book was the only thing the thieves stole.

prohibit from

Poodles are prohibited from entering delis.

protect against

A good hair conditioner can help protect against split ends.

provide with

My parents provided me with love, food, clothes, and a warm house, but not a Corvette on my sixteenth birthday.

question whether

Have you ever questioned whether you will ever be done with studying?

range from [1] to [2]

The judges' scores on her ice skating performance ranged from 4.4 to 5.9.

rather than

My father would rather eat vegetables than meat.

regard as

Dr. Pantley is regarded as the foremost expert in her field.

replace with

We've secretly replaced this fine gourmet coffee with Folger's Crystals.

require of and require to

My school requires 40 hours a year of community service from each student. We are required to do community service if we want to graduate.

responsibility to

My friend has the responsibility to train for a marathon.

responsible for

She is responsible for running a certain number of miles every day.

result from and result in

Her success in running the marathon will result from her consistent training. All the miles she runs will result in a great time in the marathon.

the same as

My school schedule is the same as yours this year.

see as

We all see Ms. Carter as the best teacher in the school.

send to

My grandmother sent a package to me at camp this summer.

sense of

Her sense of style increased after she started reading *Vogue* magazine.

so . . . that

She is so pretty that she makes guys nervous.

spend on

If you start investing the money you spend on cheeseburgers each year, you could retire when you're 40.

subject to

The money you win in the lottery is subject to taxes, unfortunately.

substitute [1] for [2]

I substituted baking soda for baking powder in the cake recipe, and it came out as flat as a pancake.

suffer from

She suffered from a broken heart for exactly two days until she met her new boyfriend.

superior to

As soon as I got my driver's license I felt superior to my brother, who was still too young to drive.

suspicious of

My mother was suspicious of the man behind her in line at the ATM because he kept trying to see the buttons she was pressing.

targeted at

The Saturday morning cartoon commercials are targeted at children who can convince their parents to buy them lots of toys.

the *-er*, the *-er*

The bigger the foot, the higher the shoe size.

the use of

The use of illegal drugs is strictly prohibited during the summer program.

the way to [verb] is to [verb]

The way to walk confidently is to hold your head high and your shoulders back.

think of . . . as

I think of him as a role model.

threaten to

My mother threatened to take away my Playstation if I got another C in algebra.

train to

Despite my best efforts, I could never train my cat to bring me a can of soda.

transmit to

Once the head office tallied the results, it transmitted them to all the local offices.

try to

Our assignment was to try to drop an egg from a third-floor window without breaking it.

type of

What type of girls do you usually go out with?

use as

She forgot her purse, so she had to use her sleeve as a tissue.

view as

I viewed her comment that my dress was "so retro" as an insult.

vote for

It is your duty to vote for the candidate who you think best espouses your views.

willing to/unwilling to

I was not willing to give up sleeping in on Saturday mornings, so I quit the team.

I was unwilling to sell my baseball card collection to a collector.

worry about

If you worry about the writing test too much, you will give yourself an ulcer.

Word Formation—A Key to Word Recognition

Many English words, especially the longer and more difficult ones, are built up out of basic parts or roots. One of the most efficient ways of increasing your vocabulary is to learn some of these parts. Once you know some basic building blocks, you will find it easier to remember words you've learned and to puzzle out unfamiliar ones.

The following chart lists over 150 common word parts. Each part is defined and an example is given of a word in which it appears. Study the chart a small section at a time. When you've learned one of the building blocks, remember to look for it in your reading. See if you can think of other words in which the word part appears. Use the dictionary to check your guesses.

WORD PART	MEANING	EXAMPLE
ab, abs	from, away	*abrade*—to wear off
		absent—away, not present
act, ag	do, act, drive	*action*—a doing
		agent—one who acts for another
alter, altr	other, change	*alternate*—to switch back and forth
am, ami	love, friend	*amorous*—loving
anim	mind, life, spirit	*animated*—spirited
annu, enni	year	*annual*—yearly
ante	before	*antedate*—to occur earlier
anthrop	man	*anthropology*—study of mankind
anti	against	*antiwar*—against war
arbit	judge	*arbiter*—a judge
arch	first, chief	*archetype*—first model
aud, audit, aur	hear	*auditorium*—place where performances are heard
auto	self	*automobile*—self-moving vehicle
bell	war	*belligerent*—warlike
bene, ben	good, well	*benefactor*—one who does good deeds

bi	two	*bilateral*—two-sided
bibli	book	*bibliophile*—book lover
bio	life	*biology*—study of life
brev	short	*abbreviate*—to shorten
cad, cas	fall	*casualty*—one who has fallen
cede, ceed, cess	go, yield	*exceed*—go beyond
		recession—a going backward
cent	hundred	*century*—hundred years
chrom	color	*monochrome*—having one color
chron	time	*chronology*—time order
cide, cis	cut, kill	*suicide*—a self-killing
		incision—a cutting into
circum	around	*circumnavigate*—to sail around
clam, claim	shout	*proclaim*—to declare loudly
clin	slope, lean	*decline*—to slope downward
cogn	know	*recognize*—to know
com, co, col, con	with, together	*concentrate*—to bring closer together
		cooperate—to work with
contra, contro, counter	against	*contradict*—to speak against
		counterclockwise—against the clock's direction
corp body	body	*incorporate*—to bring into a
cosm	order, world	*cosmos*—universe
cre, cresc	grow	*increase*—to grow
cred	trust, believe	*incredible*—unbelievable
culp	blame	*culprit*—one who is to blame
cur, curr, curs	run, course	*current*—presently running
de	away from, down, opposite	*detract*—to draw away from
dec	ten	*decade*—ten years

dem	people	*democracy*—rule by the people
dic, dict	say, speak	*dictation*—a speaking
		predict—to say in advance
dis, di	not, away from	*dislike*—to not like
		digress—to turn away from the subject
doc, doct	teach, prove	*indoctrinate*—to teach
domin	rule	*domineer*—to rule over
du	two	*duo*—a couple
duc, duct	lead	*induct*—to lead in
dur	hard, lasting	*durable*—able to last
equ	equal	*equivalent*—of equal value
ev	time, age	*longevity*—age, length of life
ex, e, ef	from, out	*expatriate*—one who lives out side his native country
		emit—to send out
extra	outside, beyond	*extraterrestrial*—from beyond the earth
fac, fact, fect, fic	do, make	*factory*—place where things are made
		fictitious—made up or ima ginary
fer	bear, carry	*transfer*—to carry across
fid	belief, faith	*fidelity*—faithfulness
fin	end, limit	*finite*—limited
flect, flex	bend	*reflect*—to bend back
flu, fluct, flux	flow	*fluid*—flowing substance
		influx—a flowing in
fore	in front of,	*forecast*—to tell ahead of previous time
		foreleg—front leg
form	shape	*formation*—shaping
fort	strong	*fortify*—to strengthen

frag, fract	break	*fragile*—easily broken
fug	flee	*fugitive*—one who flees
gen	birth, kind, race	*engender*—to give birth to
geo	earth	*geology*—study of the earth
grad, gress	step, go	*progress*—to go forward
graph	writing	*autograph*—to write one's own name
her, hes	stick, cling	*adhere*—to cling
		cohesive—sticking together
homo	same, like	*homophonic*—sounding the same
hyper	too much, over	*hyperactive*—overly active
in, il, ig, im, ir	not	*incorrect*—not correct
		ignorant—not knowing
		illogical—not logical
		irresponsible—not responsible
in, il, im, ir	on, into, in	*impose*—to place on
		invade—to go into
inter	between, among	*interplanetary*—between planets
intra, intro	within, inside	*intrastate*—within a state
ject	throw	*reject*—to throw back
junct	join	*juncture*—place where things join
leg	law	*legal*—lawful
leg, lig, lect	choose, gather,	*legible*—readable read *eligible*—able to be chosen
		select—to choose
lev	light, rise	*alleviate*—to make lighter
liber	free	*liberation*—a freeing
loc	place	*location*—place
log	speech, study	*dialogue*—speech for two characters
		psychology—study of the mind

luc, lum	light	*translucent*—allowing some light to pass through
		luminous—shining
magn	large, great	*magnify*—to make larger
mal, male	bad, wrong, poor	*maladjusted*—poorly adjusted
		malevolent—ill-wishing
mar	sea	*marine*—sea-dwelling
ment	mind	*demented*—out of one's mind
meter, metr, mens	measure	*chronometer*—time-measuring device
		commensurate—of equal measure
micr	small	*microwave*—small wave
min	little	*minimum*—least
mis	badly, wrongly	*misunderstand*—to understand wrongly
mit, miss	send	*remit*—to send back
		mission—a sending
mono	single, one	*monorail*—train that runs on a single track
morph	shape	*anthropomorphic*—man-shaped
mov, mob, mot	move	*removal*—a moving away
		mobile—able to move
multi	many	*multiply*—to become many
mut	change	*mutation*—change
nasc, nat	born	*innate*—inborn
		native—belonging by or from birth
neg	deny	*negative*—no, not
neo	new	*neophyte*—beginner
nom	name	*nominate*—to name for office
non	not	*nonentity*—a nobody
nov	new	*novice*—newcomer, beginner
		innovation—something new

omni	all	*omnipresent*—present in all places
oper	work	*operate*—to work
		cooperation—a working together
path, pat, pass	feel, suffer	*patient*—suffering
		compassion—a feeling with
ped, pod	foot	*pedestrian*—one who goes on foot
pel, puls	drive, push	*impel*—to push
phil	love	*philosophy*—love of wisdom
phob	fear	*phobia*—irrational fear
phon	sound	*symphony*—a sounding together
phot	light	*photosynthesis*—synthesis of chemical compounds in plants with the aid of light
poly	many	*polygon*—many-sided figure
port	carry	*import*—to carry into a country
pot	power	*potency*—power
post	after	*postmortem*—after death
pre	before, earlier than	*prejudice*—judgment in advance
press	press	*impression*—a pressing into
prim	first	*primal*—first, original
pro	infavor of, in front of, forward	*proceed*—to go forward
		prowar—in favor of war
psych	mind	*psychiatry*—cure of the mind
quer, quir, quis, ques	ask, seek	*query*—to ask
		inquisitive—asking many questions
		quest—a search

Grammar Essentials for the Pre-GED Student

re	back, again	*rethink*—to think again
		reimburse—to pay back
rid, ris	laugh	*deride*—to make fun of
		ridiculous—laughable
rupt	break	*erupt*—to break out
sci, scio	know	*science*—knowledge
		conscious—having knowledge
scrib, script	write	*describe*—to write about
		inscription—a writing on
semi	half	*semiconscious*—half conscious
sent, sens	feel, think	*sensation*—feeling
		sentimental—marked by feeling
sequ, secut	follow	*sequential*—following in order
sol	alone	*desolate*—lonely
solv, solu, solut	loosen	*dissolve*—to loosen the bonds of
		solvent—loosening agent
son	sound	*sonorous*—sounding
spect	look	*inspect*—to look into
		spectacle—something to be looked at
spir	breathe	*respiration*—breathing
stab, stat	stand	*establish*—to make stand, found
string, strict	bind	*restrict*—to bind, limit
stru, struct	build	*construct*—to build
super	over, greater	*superfluous*—overflowing beyond what is needed
tang, ting, tact, tig	touch	*tactile*—of the sense of touch
		contiguous—touching
tele	far	*television*—machine for seeing far

ten, tain, tent	hold	*tenacity*—holding power
		contain—to hold together
term	end	*terminal*—last, ending
terr	earth	*terrain*—surface of the earth
test	witness	*attest*—to witness
therm	heat	*thermos*—container that retains heat
tort, tors	twist	*contort*—to twist out of shape
tract	pull, draw	*attract*—to pull toward
trans	across	*transport*—to carry across a distance
un	not	*uninformed*—not informed
uni	one	*unify*—to make one
vac	empty	*evacuate*—to make empty
ven, vent	come	*convene*—to come together
ver	true	*verity*—truth
verb	word	*verbose*—wordy
vid, vis	see	*video*—means of seeing
		vision—sight
viv, vit	life	*vivid*—lively
voc, vok	call	*provocative*—calling for a response
		revoke—to call back
vol	wish, will	*involuntary*—not willed

Test-Taking Tips and Strategies C

I. Prepare Your Mind

Being mentally ready to take a test is very important. You must walk into any test with a positive mental attitude. YOU CAN DO IT!

This should be easy. You've studied this book, and maybe others. You're comfortable with the material on the test. You won't run into any surprises. So take some deep breaths and walk into the test room knowing that you can succeed!

Be relaxed. Be confident.

II. The Night Before

Cramming doesn't work for any kind of test. So the night before the test, you should briefly review some of the concepts that you're still unsure of. Then go straight to bed. Make sure you get enough sleep. You'll be glad you did the next morning.

III. The Morning of the Test

Did you know that you think better when you have a full stomach? So don't skip breakfast the morning of the test. Get to your test site early (you should make a practice run before the test if the test site is in an unfamiliar area).

Come prepared with all the materials you'll need. These might include number 2 pencils or identification. You might want to wear a watch too, in case the room you're in doesn't have a clock.

IV. Test Time

Before the test begins, make sure you have everything you need. This will keep your test anxiety low.

Choose a comfortable seat (if possible) in a spot where you will not be distracted, cold, hot, etc.

Try not to talk to other test-takers before the test. Anxiety is contagious.

V. Managing Time

Scan through the test quickly before starting it. Be familiar with the time for each section and the time the test should be over. Look at how many questions there are, and where the answers are filled in.

READ ALL DIRECTIONS VERY CAREFULLY.

VI. Know Your Test

On the GED, test questions are arranged in order of difficulty. This means the easier questions come first. So the more time you spend on the easier early questions, the less time you'll have for the harder questions later in the section. If you're stuck, don't get worried or frustrated. Circle the question and move on. Go back to it later, once you've finished the rest of the test. And make sure that you skip space on the answer documents for every question you skip on the test.

VII. Test Review

Once you've finished taking the test, look back over the exam to review what you've done. Resist the urge to run away as fast as you can once you mark your last answer. Some things to look for:

Make sure you've answered all the questions.

Proofread (when you're doing any written work).

Check your math for careless mistakes (when you're doing any math sections).

Answer any questions you skipped.

Good luck!

Notes

Notes

Notes

Notes